UNUSUALLY

GRADE **4**

BEAR LAWS

FUNNY FACE COMPETITION

1st

CONSTRUCTION EQUIPMENT

THEME PARK

READING & MATH

SERIOUSLY FUN TOPICS TO TEACH
SERIOUSLY IMPORTANT SKILLS

T0016651

Carson Dellosa Education
Greensboro, North Carolina

The facts presented in this book are for informational and entertainment purposes only. The nature of extreme facts makes them difficult to authenticate. Carson Dellosa Education makes no warranty as to the reliability, accuracy, timeliness, usefulness, or completeness of the facts contained herein.

Credits
Authors: Chris Schwab, Jennifer Stith, Hailey Scragg
Cover Design: Joshua Janes
Interior Design: Joshua Janes, Lynne Schwaner

Carson Dellosa Education
PO Box 35665
Greensboro, NC 27425
carsondellosa.com

ISBN 978-1-4838-6713-7

TABLE OF CONTENTS

A RHUMBA OF RATTLESNAKES

We've all heard of a swarm of ants, a litter of puppies, or a herd of buffalo. But, a murder of crows? A pandemonium of parrots? Collective animal names are fun. Some make sense, but others don't. If you spot a group of rattlesnakes all tangled together, you have seen a rhumba, which is also the name for a kind of dance. Calling a group of wiggling snakes a *rhumba* makes sense!

Take a look at this list and see if you can figure out how these animal groups got their names.

Animal Group	Collective Name
walruses	huddle
rhinos	crash
alligators	congregation
hippos	thunder
leopards	leap
rats	mischief
porcupines	prickle
lemurs	conspiracy
owls	parliament
giraffes	tower

FUN FACT

A group of bees may be called a swarm, a nest, a drift, a colony, a hive, a rabble, a grist, or a cluster. But, it is more fun when they are called a *bike* of bees!

Match each animal group to its collective name.

1. rhinos   a murder

2. alligators   a crash

3. crows   a prickle

4. porcupines   a congregation

Answer each question.

5. Why do you think a group of owls is called a *parliament*?

_____

_____

_____

6. What is a good collective name for a group of squirrels? Explain.

_____

_____

5

Solve each problem.

1. Two trees each have a pandemonium of parrots in them. In the first tree, there are 730 parrots. In the second tree, there are 265 parrots. If the two groups join together, how many parrots would be in the pandemonium?

_____ parrots

2. A bike of 1,803 bees are buzzing in a meadow. An additional 1,104 bees join them. How many bees are in the meadow now?

_____ bees

3. A murder of 99 crows are resting in a cemetery. If 58 of the crows fly away, then how many crows are in the murder now?

_____ crows

4. A mischief of 903 rats are scuttling about in the sewer. If 336 of the rats go above ground to search for food, then how many rats are left in the sewer?

_____ rats

Read the clues about a conspiracy of lemurs and answer the question.

Question: Who ate the bananas?

- Julien didn't eat flowers or insects for lunch.

- Marie ate flowers and insects for lunch.

- Andry had the same lunch as either Marie or Tiana.

- Zo ate only flowers for lunch.

- Tiana is the only one who ate bird eggs for lunch.

	bananas	flowers	insects	bird eggs
JULIEN				
MARIE				
ANDRY				
ZO				
TIANA				

Answer: _____

MR. BLOBBY

The poor blobfish, aka fathead sculpin, has been called "the world's ugliest animal." It certainly can't compete with kittens or panda bears for cuteness. Or anything else, for that matter. But there's more here than meets the eye.

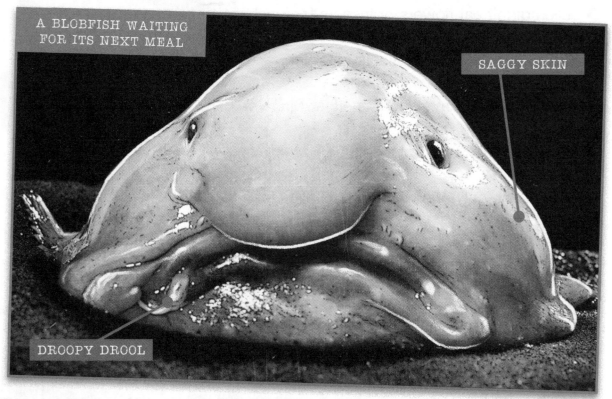

A BLOBFISH WAITING FOR ITS NEXT MEAL

SAGGY SKIN

DROOPY DROOL

The blobfish is a deep-water fish that lives in the bottom pockets of the Atlantic, Indian, and Pacific Oceans. It is found off the coasts of Australia, Tasmania, and New Zealand. A blobfish is pinkish in color and weighs no more than about 20 pounds. A blobfish has no skeleton, only a few soft bones. With no muscles to speak of, it sags. It has a large head. Its skin droops. It's a blob!

This body works for the blobfish. It's at home very far down in the ocean. Human bones would be crushed at such depths. Because it is more like a blob of jelly than anything else, it doesn't need a skeleton. It can just float across the ocean floor. It uses very little energy to live.

 **FUN FACT** The blobfish is so lazy it does not hunt for food. It just eats whatever drifts in front of its mouth!

1. The blobfish does not live in which ocean?

   A. Pacific

   B. Indian

   C. Arctic

   D. Atlantic

I HOPE THAT MR. BLOBBY DOESN'T CATCH MY DRIFT!

2. According to the text, this fish is called a blobfish because it

   A. is round.

   B. has no skeleton, so its body sags.

   C. has a large head.

   D. weighs no more than 20 pounds.

Write a response to each question.

3. Do you agree that the blobfish is "the world's ugliest animal"? Explain.

   _____

   _____

4. Why do you think the author called the blobfish *lazy*? Support your answer with evidence from the text.

   _____

   _____

Choose the best unit of measure for each object.

The blobfish weighs about 20 pounds. The pound is a unit in the standard system for measuring weight. Other units in this system are the ounce and ton.

16 ounces = 1 pound	2,000 pounds = 1 ton

1. whale   ounce   pound   ton

2. seal   ounce   pound   ton

3. clam   ounce   pound   ton

4. yacht   ounce   pound   ton

Solve each problem. Remember, a blobfish weighs about 20 pounds.

5. In one section of the ocean, there are 200 pounds of blobfish. About how many blobfish are in that section of the ocean?

_____ blobfish

6. In another section of the ocean, there are 2,000 pounds of blobfish. About how many blobfish are in that section of the ocean?

_____ blobfish

Help the blobfish find some food. Write the letters the blobfish passes in order on the lines below to finish the fun fact.

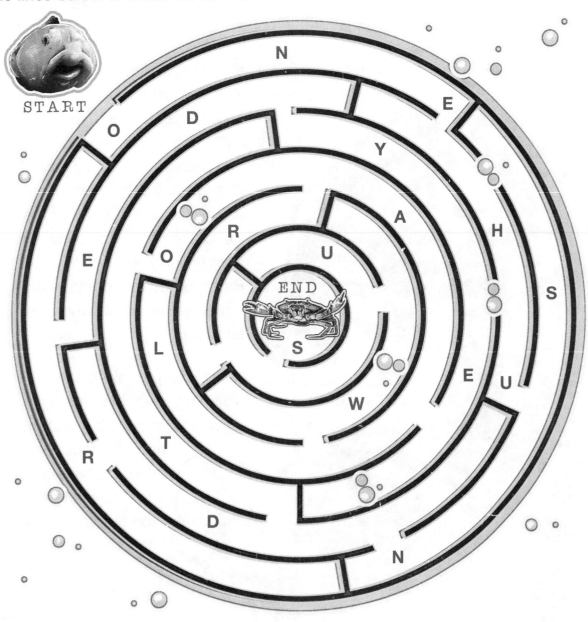

The life expectancy of the blobfish is not known, but scientists speculate it is pretty long! Many deepwater creatures live more than

_____ _____ _____

_____ _____ _____ _____

_____ _____ _____ .

Let's talk about barf. Did you know rabbits cannot vomit? They cannot gag, and they cannot throw up. Poor bunnies. What happens when their stomachs are upset? Or if they have swallowed something poisonous? Or if a hairball is stuck?

A rabbit's digestive system is different from yours. When humans eat bad food or if they have a virus, throwing up helps keep them safe. But, everything a rabbit eats stays down. Rabbits graze. They eat all day, off and on. So, their stomachs are usually full. A band at the top of the stomach keeps acid from leaking out. That's good. But, food cannot come back out either, not even when it's bad food.

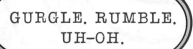

GURGLE. RUMBLE. UH-OH.

Sickness Bag

Keep your pet rabbit safe by watching everything it eats. Keep it away from anything that might be poisonous. Brush your rabbit regularly so it doesn't swallow too much of its own hair when it grooms itself. And, take it to a vet when it is sick.

FUN FACT

Rabbits cannot vomit. But they can cough, and they can sneeze! *Gesundheit!*

Write a response to each question.

1. Write two synonyms for the word *barf* from the text.

_____   _____

2. According to the text, what can you do to keep rabbits safe?

_____

_____

_____

Match each word to its definition.

3. graze   something that causes harm when eaten

4. digestion   to eat small amounts often

5. acid   the process of breaking down food

6. poisonous   a sour substance, such as vinegar

I'M ALL EARS!

Find the perimeter and area of each rabbit hutch.

Perimeter is the distance around a figure. It is found by adding all the sides.
Area is the total space taken up by an object. It is found by multiplying the length times the width.

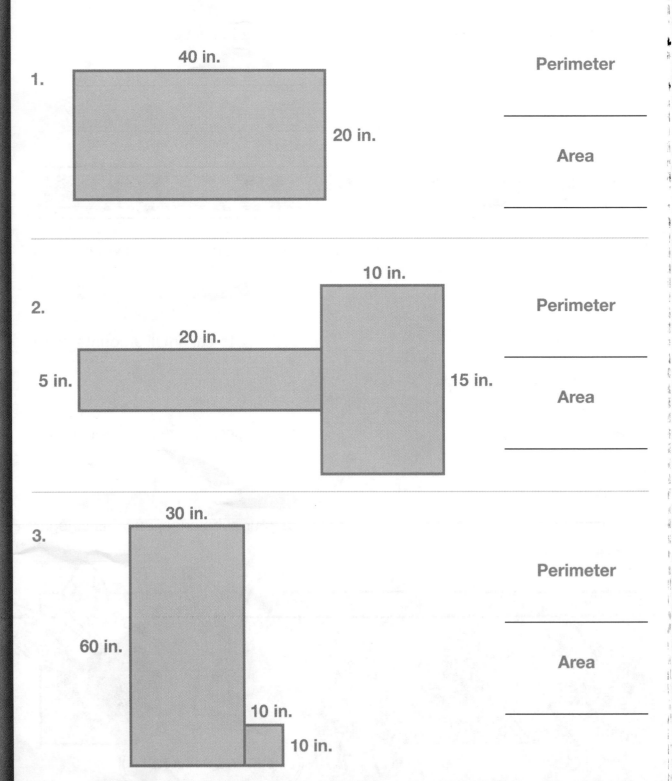

1.

40 in.

20 in.

Perimeter

_____

Area

_____

2.

10 in.

20 in.

5 in.

15 in.

Perimeter

_____

Area

_____

3.

30 in.

60 in.

10 in.

10 in.

Perimeter

_____

Area

_____

Read the clues. Look at the rabbits. Write the letter of the correct rabbit next to each clue.

A   B   C   D

Clues:

1. The *English Spot* is a breed that originated in England in the 1800s. This pretty black and white breed's best clue is in its name. _____

2. The *Angora* rabbit requires a lot of maintenance! Their fluffy long coats need frequent brushing. _____

3. These floppy-eared cuties are called *English Lops*. They're known for being calm and friendly. _____

4. The *Netherland Dwarf* is a tiny breed that weighs on average less than 2.5 pounds. Even their ears are small! _____

JOEY

FEEDING "TUBE"

A baby koala is called a *joey*. When it is born, it has no hair and looks like a pink jelly bean. It lives in its mother's pouch for about six months.

The koala baby's diet is unique. Believe it or not, baby koalas eat their mother's poop. This sounds gross, but it is healthy. At first, the baby koala drinks only its mother's milk. But then, when its eyes open, it sticks its head outside the pouch. It tickles its mom's bottom. It is ready for more solid food.

The mother koala drops some pellets too but feeds the baby a runnier kind of poop called *pap*. Pap is high in protein and helps the baby koala grow. It also helps the joey get ready for an adult meal of eucalyptus leaves. Eucalyptus leaves are hard to digest and can be poisonous. The mother has bacteria in her stomach to help digest them. These bacteria are passed on into the baby's digestive system when it eats her poop.

PEAK-A-POO!

FUN FACT Human babies go from milk to baby food in jars to solid food. It is the same for baby koalas, only their baby food is called *pap*. And it does not come in a jar!

1. Do you think the title for this passage is a good one? Explain.

_____

_____

2. Find the simile in this passage. What two things are compared?

_____

_____

3. How does bacteria from the mother help the joey?

_____

Write two antonyms for each word from the text.

4. baby _____

5. unique _____

6. gross _____

7. healthy _____

Solve each problem.

1. In a eucalyptus forest, there are 16 joeys. If 8 of the joeys drink milk, and 8 of the joeys eat pap, then what fraction of joeys drink milk?

Look at the pie chart. What is another way you can write the fraction of joeys that drink milk?

Joeys' Diet

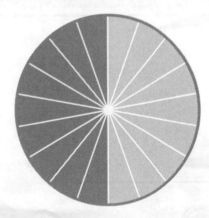

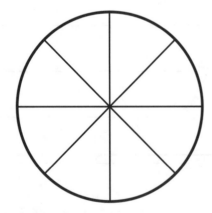

■ Joeys that drink milk

■ Joeys that eat pap

2. In another forest, there are 8 joeys. There are 2 joeys drinking milk, and 6 eating pap. Color the pie chart to show the fraction of joeys that are drinking milk. Write the fraction in simplest form.

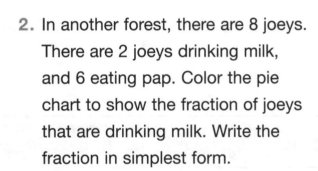

☐ Joeys that drink milk

☐ Joeys that eat pap

Koalas are found in Australia. Find the names of 10 other Australian animals hidden in the puzzle.

DINGO   TASMANIAN DEVIL

KANGAROO   EMU

WOMBAT   SUGAR GLIDER

QUOKKA   WALLABY

PLATYPUS   ECHIDNA

A	G	W	R	T	U	M	G	Y	X	C	G	R	L
O	K	A	N	G	A	R	O	O	A	G	U	I	W
M	P	L	A	T	Y	P	U	S	E	H	V	L	T
J	F	L	S	B	C	X	S	D	T	E	O	M	S
S	D	A	Y	A	E	M	U	F	D	J	A	B	R
E	R	B	H	L	J	A	G	N	O	I	I	C	Q
E	L	Y	G	M	K	E	A	L	M	L	N	Z	Q
Q	B	C	N	X	S	I	R	W	X	B	E	G	U
W	N	Z	P	E	N	O	G	C	D	X	H	L	O
O	X	Y	Q	A	R	N	L	X	Y	Y	K	J	K
M	A	K	M	T	K	M	I	N	V	D	T	G	K
B	J	S	V	U	O	A	D	E	J	F	S	D	A
A	A	O	D	I	P	Z	E	C	H	I	D	N	A
T	T	S	W	U	W	C	R	S	I	K	L	A	C

KNOCKOUT!

The peacock mantis shrimp is beautiful, colored in a rainbow of red, blue, orange, and green. But don't be fooled by its beauty. It can throw a punch to beat any boxing legend. And it's barely six inches long! This creature is not a shrimp or a mantis. Its family name is *stomatopod* or *crustacean*.

The mantis shrimp has super eyesight, with two big eyes on stems. The eyes can work together or by themselves. Watch them swivel on the hunt! These eyes can see more colors than any other creature, so the mantis shrimp is good at spotting its favorite foods such as clams, crabs, and other shellfish.

Once its prey is within reach, the mantis shrimp flies through the water and attacks the shell of its prey. It lets loose in a fury with its two front hammer claws. It punches faster than a human can blink. Whack! Wham! Pow! Crack! The shell is broken. Dinner is ready!

FUN FACT

The mantis shrimp's punch goes about 60 miles an hour (96 km/h) and has been compared to a speeding bullet.

1. What is the meaning of the word *swivel* in the text?

   A. to move from side to side and up and down

   B. to look straight ahead

   C. to disappear

2. Which quality does not help the peacock mantis shrimp capture its prey?

   A. its big eyes

   B. its rainbow colors

   C. its hammer claws

   D. its speedy punch

Write a response to each question.

3. Write four examples of onomatopoeia in the text.

   _____   _____

   _____   _____

4. Write four adjectives the author uses to describe the peacock mantis shrimp.

   _____   _____

   _____   _____

Solve each problem.

1. If 7 peacock mantis shrimp each punch 66 clams, then how many total clams get punched?

_____ clams

2. If 8 peacock mantis shrimp each punch 51 crabs, then how many total crabs get punched?

_____ crabs

3. If 4 peacock mantis shrimp punch a total of 56 clams, then how many clams does each peacock mantis shrimp punch if they all punch the same number of clams?

_____ clams

4. A peacock mantis shrimp punches 72 crabs in 6 days. How many crabs does the peacock mantis shrimp punch each day?

_____ crabs

Follow the directions.

Help the peacock mantis shrimp find its next victim. Write the letters it passes in order on the lines below to finish the fun fact.

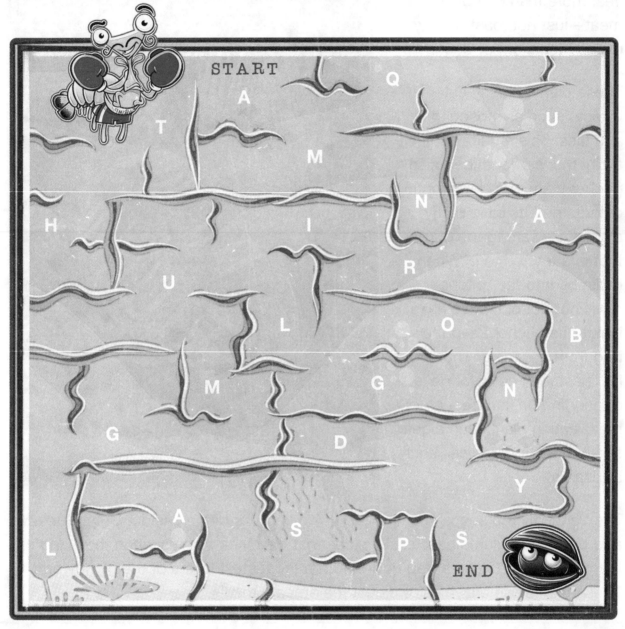

A peacock mantis shrimp would be a risky creature to keep in your fish tank.
Their punches are so strong, they can break

_____ _____ _____ _____ _____ _____

_____ _____ _____ _____ _____ !

WHERE'S THE BEEF?

Meat-eating plants? Really? Yes, more than 600 plants eat meat—just not roast turkey, grilled steak, or hot dogs.

These plants mostly eat insects such as mosquitoes and flies. This requires some tricky moves. Take the Asian pitcher plant, with its tempting colorful rim. Its lid is partly closed. Beware to the bug that is attracted to it. When it climbs into the "pitcher," it will not get out! Little hairs inside the pitcher keep the bug from escaping. The bug is digested in hours or days, depending on its size. Larger meat-eating plants can digest small rodents or reptiles such as lizards.

A VENUS FLYTRAP SECRETES NECTAR TO ATTRACT INSECTS. ONCE INSIDE, THE INSECT TRIGGERS SMALL HAIRS THAT CAUSE THE LOBES TO SNAP SHUT AND IMPRISON THE INSECT.

The Venus flytrap snaps shut like a clam to keep its dinner inside! Gulp! Sundew and butterwort plants have sticky sides that trap their victims when they land on them. Butterworts use a trap door and are the fastest killers of the plant world. These plants use enzymes to digest their meaty meals.

 **FUN FACT**

A newly discovered pitcher plant in Indonesia uses underground traps. This clever plant traps and eats insects, such as ants, that live or travel underground.

Complete each sentence with a word from the word bank.

attracted	digest	escaping	tempting	underground

1. Enzymes help the plants _____ their meals.

2. Insects are _____ to colorful plants.

3. The Asian pitcher plant has a _____, colorful rim.

4. Little hairs keep the bugs from _____.

5. A newly discovered plant traps ants _____.

Write a response to the question.

6. What do you think about meat-eating plants? Explain.

_____

_____

C'MERE LITTLE BUGGY...

Solve each problem.

1. A pitcher plant catches $\frac{3}{4}$ of the bugs that land on it. A Venus flytrap catches an equivalent fraction of bugs. If 16 bugs land on the Venus flytrap what fraction of bugs does the Venus flytrap catch?

2. A butterwort plant eats 10 bugs. Eight of the bugs are flies. A Venus flytrap eats an equivalent fraction of flies. If the Venus flytrap eats 5 bugs, what fraction of the bugs eaten were flies?

_____ bugs

_____ flies

Use the table to answer each question.

Day	Monday	Tuesday	Wednesday	Thursday	Friday
Fraction of Bugs Caught	$\frac{3}{4}$	$\frac{3}{6}$	$\frac{3}{8}$	$\frac{6}{8}$	$\frac{4}{8}$

3. On which day did the plant catch an equivalent fraction of bugs as it did on Tuesday?

_____

4. On which day did the plant catch an equivalent fraction of bugs as it did on Thursday?

_____

1	2	3	4	5	6	7	8	9	10	11	12	13
A	B	C	D	E	F	G	H	I	J	K	L	M

14	15	16	17	18	19	20	21	22	23	24	25	26
N	O	P	Q	R	S	T	U	V	W	X	Y	Z

Pitcher plants aren't always out to eat creatures!
In fact, they have a special relationship with one animal. Pitcher plants

___ ___ ___ ___ ___ ___ ___
16 18 15 22 9   4   5

___ ___ ___ ___ ___ ___ ___   ___ ___ ___
19 8   5   12 20 5   18   6   15 18

___ ___ ___ ___   ___ ___
2   1   20 19   9   14

___ ___ ___ ___ ___ ___ ___ ___
5   24 3   8   1   14 7   5

___ ___ ___   ___ ___ ___ ___ ___
6   15 18   20 8   5   9   18

___ ___ ___ ___,
16 15 15 16

which the pitcher plants use as nourishment!

NOM,
NOM

The jellyfish is nearly 98 percent water. It has no brain, heart, lungs, or blood. Still, it can swim great oceans, eat dinner, and even sting people!

Jellyfish have been around for 600 million years. Scientists have named 2,000 species but think more than 300,000 exist. One species may even be immortal, meaning it never dies. When it is scared, starving, sick, or old, it can change itself back into a baby jellyfish. It just resets its cells. But most jellyfish aren't that lucky. Some live for a year, others for only a few days.

Jellyfish have stingers in their tentacles that paralyze their prey. They like to eat shrimp, crabs, fish, and tiny plants. Then, like most other creatures, they need to poop. The warty comb jellyfish is unusual. Each time it poops, its butt disappears! A new one grows whenever it needs to poop again.

FUN FACT

Some jellyfish have names that match their appearance, such as pink meanie jellyfish and fried egg jellyfish.

SOME JELLYFISH EMIT LIGHT TO DEFEND AGAINST PREDATORS. THIS IS CALLED BIOLUMINESCENCE.

Write a response to the question.

1. If all creatures, including people, were immortal, would this be a good or bad thing? Explain.

_____

_____

_____

Match each word to its definition.

2. sting   to make unable to feel or move

3. species   a long, thin armlike part, usually on a head or mouth

4. tentacle   to hurt or stick with a stinger

5. paralyze   a group of living things that are alike in most ways

THE "JELLY" ROGER

Solve each problem.

1. Scientists have identified 2,000 species of jellyfish but think more than 300,000 exist. If this is true, how many species of jellyfish have yet to be discovered?

_____ species

2. One species of jellyfish can turn itself back into a baby. If a jellyfish appears to be 13 years old but has lived for 4 times that long, how many years has the jellyfish been alive?

_____ years

3. A jellyfish has lived for 86 years. If it appears to be half that old, how old does the jellyfish appear to be?

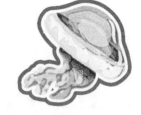

_____ years old

4. Collectively, a group of 8 jellyfish have 568 years between them. If each jellyfish is the same age, how old are they?

_____ years old

Help the jellyfish find its friends. Follow the numbers that are factors of 60.

Most animals (and people) pee several times a day. When you have to go, you have to go! But that's not true for a certain wood frog found in Alaska and all over Canada. It can hold its pee for up to eight months. That's nearly 250 days!

FUN FACT When a wood frog freezes, two-thirds of its body turns to ice. You could not bend one of its legs without breaking it off.

These hardy creatures freeze solid in the frigid Alaskan temperatures of zero and below. They are like little rocks. They are hard to see. Their eyes are white, and their skin is solid. Their heart, brain, and bloodstream stop. If they were mammals, they would be dead.

During the long, cold winter, part of their pee turns into nitrogen. Special gut bacteria make this happen. This nitrogen flows through the body all winter long as the wood frog hibernates. It keeps their cells and tissues alive. Then, when spring arrives, they quickly thaw out and hop away.

Answer each question.

1. Where does the wood frog in the text live?

   A. Parts of South America

   B. Alaska and Canada

   C. Antarctica

   D. Russia

   > BRRRR–IBBIT!

2. According to the text, what does not happen to these wood frogs in the winter?

   A. They freeze solid.

   B. Their eyes are white.

   C. Their heart, brain, and bloodstream stop.

   D. They pee several times a day.

Complete each sentence with a word from the word bank.

bacteria	frigid	hibernate

3. Winter weather in Alaska brings _____ temperatures.

4. Special gut _____ help wood frogs hold their pee.

5. Many creatures _____ during the winter months.

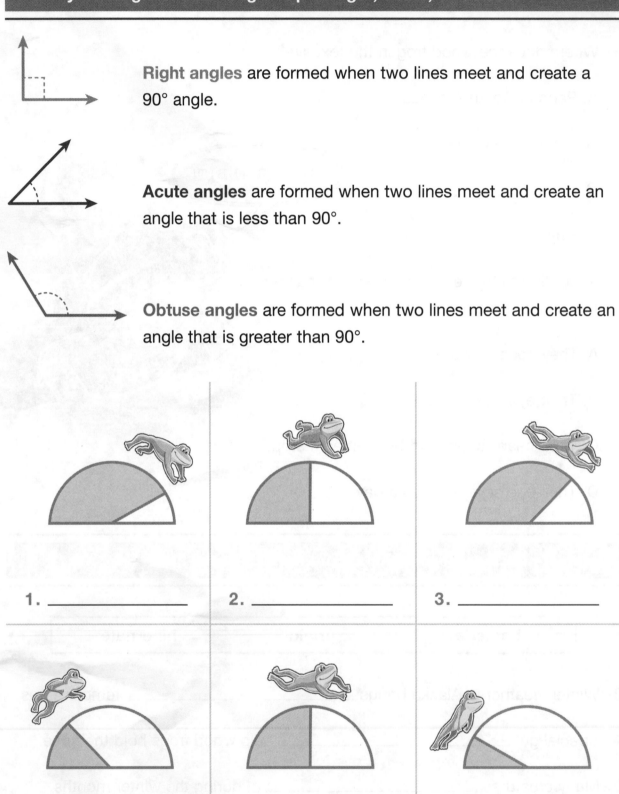

Right angles are formed when two lines meet and create a 90° angle.

Acute angles are formed when two lines meet and create an angle that is less than 90°.

Obtuse angles are formed when two lines meet and create an angle that is greater than 90°.

1. _____

2. _____

3. _____

4. _____

5. _____

6. _____

Use the words in the word bank to solve the crossword puzzle clues about other frog species.

| blue poison dart | tomato | desert rain |
| Amazon milk | American bullfrog | goliath |

ACROSS

3. The ____ frog is speckled brown and white. It secretes a milky looking substance from its skin when it is scared or stressed.

5. The ____'s croak is deep and loud, and some think it sounds like a cow's moo.

6. The ____ frog buries itself in sand during the day to stay cool.

DOWN

1. The ____ frog can weigh from 1 to 7 pounds, making it the largest frog in the world!

2. The ____ frog has beautiful blue skin. But watch out! That skin is dangerous and secretes poison.

4. The ____ frog is plump and red and lives in tropical rain forests.

With its red lips and four "legs," you might say the red-lipped batfish looks more like a pouting puppy than a fish. But it is definitely a fish! This odd-looking bottom dweller can be found in coral reefs in the Pacific Ocean. They are mostly spotted around the Galapagos Islands, west of northern South America.

A BATFISH "WALKING" ON ITS FINS.

FUN FACT

The red-lipped batfish uses its fins to swim, but it often stops and appears to perch or walk on its fins as if they are legs.

The body of the batfish is plain, mostly tan and gray with darker brown spots. Its horn and snout are a shade of brown. But, its lips make the fish stand out! If you didn't know better, you would think it had just rubbed on a coat of bright red lipstick. Is it ready to party? No one knows for sure, but scientists think the colorful lips help the batfish find a mate.

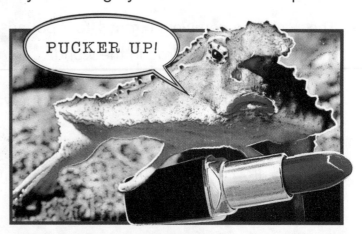

PUCKER UP!

Answer each question.

1. Which is the meaning of the word *plain* as used in the passage?

   A. a machine that flies

   B. easily understood

   C. not pretty

   D. a flat area without many trees

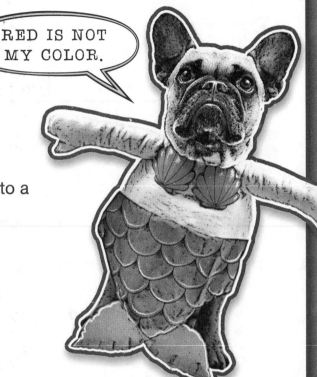

RED IS NOT MY COLOR.

2. Why did the author compare the batfish to a pouting puppy?

   A. Its tail wags like a dog's tail.

   B. It appears to have four legs.

   C. It barks.

   D. It can do tricks.

Write a response to each question.

3. The author says the batfish is plain. Write three supporting details.

   _____

   _____

   _____

4. Write a different title for this passage.

   _____

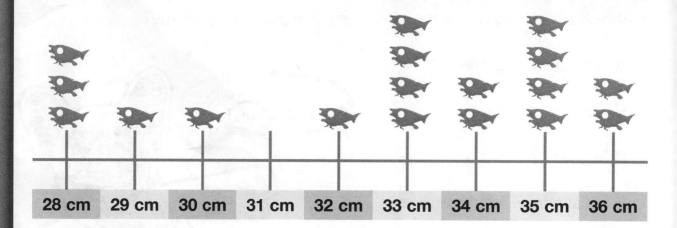

| 28 cm | 29 cm | 30 cm | 31 cm | 32 cm | 33 cm | 34 cm | 35 cm | 36 cm |

1. How many batfish are 33 cm long? _____

2. How many batfish are 28 cm long? _____

3. Which measurements had two batfish that size? _____

   and _____

4. What is the difference in length between the shortest and longest batfish?

   _____

5. Which measurements had the most batfish that size? _____

   and _____

6. How many total batfish were measured? _____

Help the batfish make its way across the ocean floor. Color the boxes that contain multiples of 3.

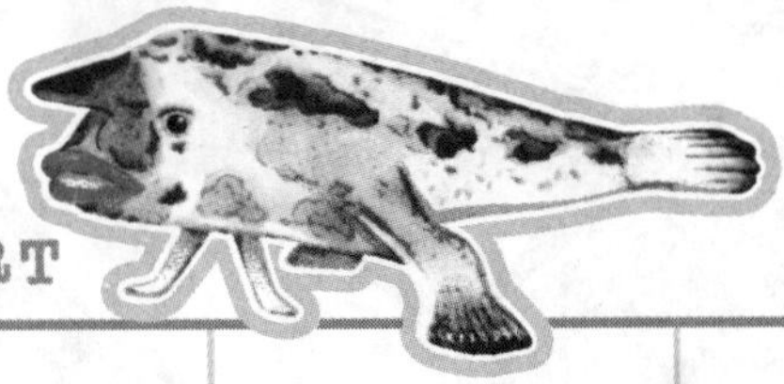

START

6	16	24	27	30
9	14	21	32	33
12	15	18	35	36
19	22	25	38	39
32	37	31	40	42

FINISH

The world record for the fastest-growing plant goes to a type of bamboo. It can grow up to 35 inches (91 cm) in a day. That's like growing as tall as a three-year-old child in one day!

Most plants take their time. But, bamboo is not the only plant with amazing growth spurts. Some trees shoot up almost overnight. The poplar tree provides awesome shade. It grows 5 to 8 feet (1.5–2.4 m) a year. Growing at a rate of 3 feet (1 m) a year is a tree nicknamed *Green Giant*. Can you guess how it got its name?

POPLAR TREE

At the other end of the scale, a tiny plant known as duckweed grows faster than about any other for its size. Duckweed grows in freshwater in every continent except Antarctica. The plants look like tiny, green, floating seeds—about the size of a pinhead. They can double in size in a day.

FUN FACT

Rhubarb grows more than an inch a day. You can hear it pop out of the bud. Later, the stalks squeak and creak as they rub together.

A LITTLE LOUDER PLEASE!

RHUBARB

Write a response to each question.

1. What is the main idea of this text?

2. What is one supporting detail?

3. How do you think the Green Giant got its name?

Use each word in a sentence. Use the part of speech indicated.

4. spurt (n)

5. scale (n)

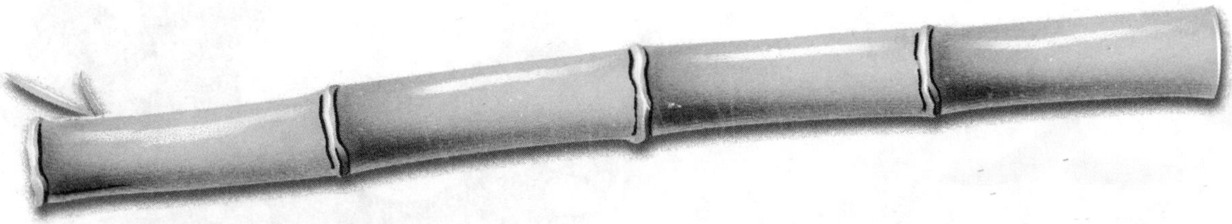

1. If a bamboo plant grows 35 inches each day for 45 days, then how many inches will it have grown in all?

_____ in.

2. If a bamboo plant grows 91 centimeters each day for 26 days, then how many centimeters will it have grown in all?

_____ cm

3. A bamboo plant grows 880 inches. If it grew 22 inches each day, then how many days did it take to grow in all?

_____ days

4. A bamboo plant grows 1,190 centimeters in 14 days. How many centimeters on average did it grow each day?

_____ cm

1	2	3	4	5	6	7	8	9	10	11	12	13
A	B	C	D	E	F	G	H	I	J	K	L	M

14	15	16	17	18	19	20	21	22	23	24	25	26
N	O	P	Q	R	S	T	U	V	W	X	Y	Z

It's a good thing bamboo grows so fast because

___ ___ ___ ___ ___ ___
16   1   14   4   1   19

___ ___ ___   ___ ___ ___
3   1   14   5   1   20

___ ___   ___ ___
21   16   20   15

___ ___ ___ ___ ___ ___ - ___ ___ ___ ___
5   9   7   8   20   25   6   15   21   18

___ ___ ___ ___ ___ ___
16   15   21   14   4   19

___   ___ ___ ___.
1   4   1   25

Do you swat off ants that climb on you? Most people do! But some birds welcome the tiny critters. They find ants helpful.

It's almost funny. Picture a robin picking up an ant in its beak. It spreads its wings and lowers its tail. It wipes the wing and tail feathers with the ant. Then, repeat! Observe a great horned owl squatting over an anthill. Like the robin, it spreads its wings and lowers its tail. The owl remains in place while the ants crawl around in its feathers. What is going on?

This is called *anting*. More than 200 kinds of birds have been seen anting. They are mostly songbirds. No one knows why for sure. But, scientists think the ants leave a smelly oil that scares away pests like biting lice and feather mites. Other scientists think the ant oils may soothe a bird's sore skin. It is possible, too, that the birds are cleaning the ants so they can then safely eat them! It's a mystery!

FUN FACT

Not just any ant will do for birds who practice anting. Only 24 species of ants, which have high levels of formic acid, are chosen.

Write a response to each question.

1. What could be another title for this passage? Explain.

_____

_____

2. What are two reasons birds may practice anting?

_____

_____

3. List the steps in order that a robin practices anting.

_____

_____

_____

_____

Write an antonym for each word from the text.

4. remains _____

5. possible _____

6. soothe _____

Robin is anting. Round each number of ants used to the nearest hundred.

1. 99 _____   124 _____

2. 255 _____   162 _____

3. 319 _____   241 _____

Owl is anting. Round each number of ants used to the nearest thousand.

4. 1,115 _____   8,091 _____

5. 6,432 _____   3,928 _____

6. 2,631 _____   7,560 _____

Help the ants find the bird! Write the letters the ants pass in order on the lines below to finish the fun fact.

Relative to their size, ants are one of the

_____ _____ _____ _____ _____ _____ _____

creatures in the world. They can carry _____ _____ _____ _____ _____

times their body weight!

Yang Tianxin, of China, loves soccer. He enjoys the sport so much he turned his fish tank into a stadium. Then, he trained his goldfish to dribble, pass, and score. Yang's goldfish can play soccer.

It probably wasn't the easiest thing Yang ever did. But, he started training them to do simple things first. He says the first thing to know about training a goldfish is to let them get to know you. Second, always reward them with food! Every time his goldfish scored a point, he gave them fish food.

Yang uses Ranchu goldfish. He says they are not very smart. It took at least three months to get any results. His goldfish lost interest in playing quite easily. But, as long as he kept feeding them, they kept learning. In six months, they were regularly scoring goals. That seems pretty smart. Go, Goldfish!

 **FUN FACT** Students at a Florida STEM university use food wands to train goldfish to play soccer. Students give them a treat when they push the ball.

Write a response to each question.

1. What two things does Yang want you to know about training goldfish?

_____

_____

2. What are three soccer skills Yang trained his goldfish to do?

_____ _____ _____

Write two meanings for each word from the passage.

3. train

_____

_____

4. score

_____

_____

Solve each problem.

(Hint: To find an average, add the quantities and then divide the sum by the number of quantities.)

1. On Monday, a goldfish touches the soccer ball 10 times. On Tuesday, the goldfish touches the ball 14 times. On Wednesday, the goldfish touches the ball 12 times. Find the average number of times the goldfish touches the ball.

   _____ times

2. A goldfish scores 2 goals on Saturday. On Sunday, the goldfish scores 5 goals. On Monday, the goldfish scores 3 goals. On Tuesday the goldfish scores 6 goals. Find the average number of goals the goldfish scores.

   _____ goals

3. A team of goldfish work on touching the ball. The team touches the ball 22 times in round one, 36 times in round two, 29 times in round three, 31 times in round four, and 32 times in round 5. What was the average number of times the team touched the ball?

   GOAL!

   _____ times

1	2	3	4	5	6	7	8	9	10	11	12	13
A	B	C	D	E	F	G	H	I	J	K	L	M

14	15	16	17	18	19	20	21	22	23	24	25	26
N	O	P	Q	R	S	T	U	V	W	X	Y	Z

Goldfish __ __ __ __ ,
       3 1 14 20

__ __ __ __ __ __ __ __ __
19 8 21 20 20 8 5 9 18

__ __ __ __ .
5 25 5 19

__ __ __ __ __ __ __ __ ,
20 8 5 25 5 15 14 20

__ __ __ __
8 1 22 5

__ __ __ __ __ __ __ !
5 25 5 12 9 4 19

The secretary bird is a large bird of prey. It stands about 4 feet (1.2 m) tall. It lives in Africa's savannahs and grasslands. It mostly moves about on foot, although it can fly. It will fly to its nest in a tree. And, it flies to show off when it is courting.

No one knows how the secretary bird got its name. Some think it's because long ago, secretaries stuck quill pens behind their ears. The bird has the same spiky feathers sticking out behind its head. Secretaries also wore long gray tailcoats and short black pants. A similar "look" can be seen on these birds.

A secretary bird is quite vicious to its prey. One of only two birds that hunt on the ground, the secretary bird eats snakes, tortoises, rats and other small rodents, amphibians, and reptiles. It especially prefers snakes and strikes the moment it sees one. Its large feet and sharp claws kick and stomp the snake to death. Some of its preferred snakes are venomous. It must kick the snake quickly and carefully before the snake bites.

FUN FACT

The secretary bird kicks hard and fast. It can kick with five times its weight in a hundredth of a second.

1. What does the author say might be a reason the secretary bird got its name? Support your answer with evidence from the text.

_____

_____

_____

2. Connect what you read about the secretary bird to another bird or animal you have read about. Explain.

_____

_____

_____

Answer the question.

3. Which of these statements tells the main idea of the third paragraph?

   A. The secretary bird has large feet and sharp claws.

   B. The secretary bird is quite vicious to its prey.

   C. The secretary bird lives in Africa.

   D. The secretary bird nests in a tree.

CAN I TAKE A MESSAGE?

Complete the graph and answer each question.

A secretary bird had a week filled with snake hunting. The number of snakes the bird caught each day is listed below.

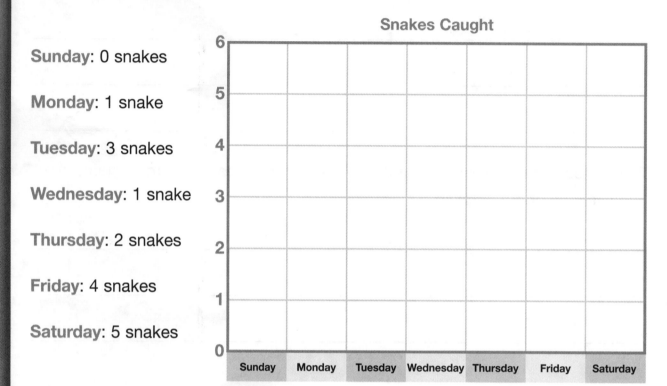

Sunday: 0 snakes

Monday: 1 snake

Tuesday: 3 snakes

Wednesday: 1 snake

Thursday: 2 snakes

Friday: 4 snakes

Saturday: 5 snakes

Snakes Caught

| | Sunday | Monday | Tuesday | Wednesday | Thursday | Friday | Saturday |

1. On which day did the bird catch twice as many snakes as it did on Thursday?

   _____

2. On which day did the bird catch three times as many snakes as it did on Monday?

   _____

3. How many total snakes did the bird catch this week?

   _____ snakes

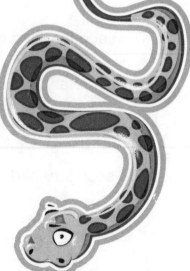

UNUSUALLY FUN READING & MATH GRADE 4

Follow the directions.

Read each clue. Cross out the letters from the words *BIRDS OF PREY*. Write the remaining letters on the lines to reveal a bird of prey.

1. Tufts of feathers called *plumicorns* sit on this bird's head and are how it got its name.

   B G I R R E D A S T O H F O P R R N E E D Y O W L

   __ __ __ __ __ __ __ __ __ __ __ __ __

2. This rare bird has a harsh habitat. It lives along the cold rocky coasts of eastern Russia.

   B S I T R E D L S L O A F R P S R S E E Y A E A G L E

   ,
   __ __ __ __ __ __ __ __ __ __ __ - __ __ __ __ __ __

3. This bird lives in the Andes Mountain range and has the largest wingspan of any raptor.

   B A I N R D D E S A O N F C P O R N E D Y O R

   __ __ __ __ __ __ __ __ __ __ __ __ __

4. These falcons are the fastest ever recorded animal, with a diving speed reaching 242 miles per hour.

   B P I E R R D E S G O R F I P N R E E F Y A L C O N

   __ __ __ __ __ __ __ __ __ __ __ __ __ __ __

5. If you've ever heard the caw of an eagle in a movie, odds are it is the actual scream of this colorful-tailed bird.

   B R I E R D D T S A O I F L P E R D E H Y A W K

   -
   __ __ __ __ __ __ __ __ __ __ __ __

You will be happy to learn this is not about worms in your ice-cream cone. Ice-cream cone worms got their name because they live in a shell that looks like an ice-cream cone.

These sea worms can be found around Central and South America. They are easily identified by their cone-shaped tubes. These are not large but can measure up to 2 inches (5 cm) long. They build their cone homes with one tiny grain of sand at a time. The hardened tube protects them.

These worms have hard hairs, like eyelashes, on top. These help them burrow headfirst into layers of sand and mud. The worms spend most of their lives facedown! They use tentacles set beside the eyelashes to poke around in the mud for food. Mixed in with soft, slimy food is sand. They swallow it all. The food digests, but all of the sand is pooped out in about six hours. Food in, sand out.

 **FUN FACT** A baby ice-cream cone worm is called a *wormlet*, just like other baby worms.

Answer each question.

1. Ice-cream cone worms live

   A. under rocks.

   B. in cone-shaped tubes.

   C. in seashells.

2. These worms can be found in

   A. Central and South America.

   B. North America.

   C. Australia.

   D. Iceland.

Write a response to each question.

3. The author said the worms "spend most of their lives facedown!" What did the author mean?

   _____

   _____

4. Draw an ice-cream cone worm in the box. Label it with adjectives from the text.

1.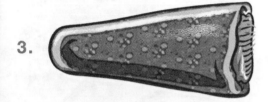

_____

2.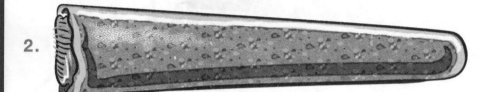

_____

3.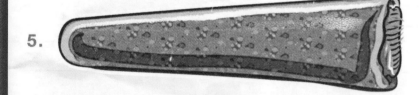

_____

4.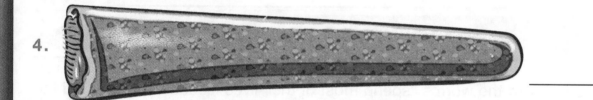

_____

5.

_____

6.

_____

Follow the directions.

Ice-cream cone worms aren't the only shelled creatures with fun names! Find other shelled creatures' names in the puzzle.

BUBBLE SHELL

EAR SHELL

HELMET SHELL

JINGLE SHELL

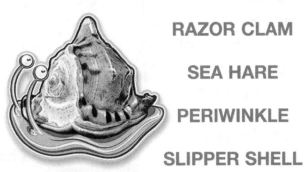

RAZOR CLAM

SEA HARE

PERIWINKLE

SLIPPER SHELL

S S V C R A Z O R C L A M G
E L M J O I E R T M K B J H
A D I S C A Z G R Y O U X N
H X Q P E R J T D J U B D L
A C V U P T E H J F K B U P
R H E L M E T S H E L L G E
E S F C G A R J N T E E H R
F R S D F R B S M P O S K I
D G V S K S L A H I U H O W
Y T R W S H D G J E L E P I
Q S V B Y E K I O T L L M N
A J I N G L E S H E L L S K
X T I Y E L M K C V J E R L
A T U C V N K J R G H U I E

AN EGG-CELLENT MEAL

The first day of spring smells like eggs in Zenica, a city in Bosnia and Herzegovina. If you look on a world map or globe, you'll find it south and east of Croatia, and west of Serbia.

Spring is said to promise new life. This community celebrates spring's promise with eggs. Every year, they hold a festival in a park by the river at the break of dawn. The festival is called *Cimburijada*, or "Festival of Scrambled Eggs." People come from all around the world to eat eggs.

Thousands of people gather to visit, dance, listen to music, and eat scrambled eggs made in huge pans. The host begins the ceremony by helping to break

thousands of eggs over big pans of butter and some secret ingredients. The scrambled eggs are free to all visitors. How egg-cellent!

FUN FACT

Restaurant owners compete to make the best scrambled eggs. One year, the winner scrambled 1,500 eggs in only one pan!

Write a response to each question.

1. The author used a pun in the title. What word is meant by "Egg-cellent"?

_____

2. Translate the festival name, *Cimburijada*, to English.

_____

3. If you were cooking a big pan of scrambled eggs, what two secret ingredients would you add?

_____

Write a sentence using each word. Use the part of speech indicated.

4. secret (*n*) _____

_____

5. promise (*v*) _____

_____

6. ingredient (*n*) _____

_____

NO CHICKENS WERE HARMED IN THE MAKING OF THESE SCRAMBLED EGGS

Solve each problem.

1. Bev and her parents went to the festival on Friday, Saturday, and Sunday. Each person ate 6 eggs on each day of the festival. How many eggs did they eat in all?

_____ eggs

2. One restaurant had 44 eggs to cook. Six eggs fit in each pan. How many pans did they need?

_____ pans

3. Another restaurant had 75 eggs to cook. Nine eggs fit in each pan. How many pans did they fill and how many eggs were left out?

_____ pans _____ eggs left out

4. One Sunday, Yuri cooked 23 eggs. Four eggs fit in his pan. How many pans of eggs did he cook?

_____ pans

George, Gina, and Gabby attended the festival. The restaurant mixed up their orders. Which order belongs to each person? Use the chart and the clues to find out!

- Gina ordered a number of eggs that is a factor of 14.

- Gabby ordered a number of eggs that is divisible by two.

- George ordered a number of eggs that is a square number.

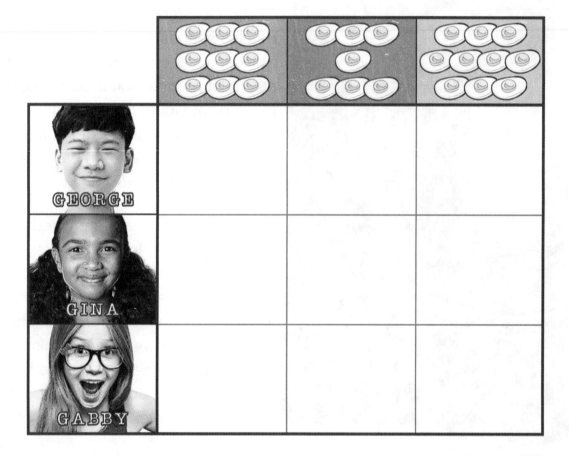

Explain your answer.

_____

_____

JOE'S GREEN THUMB

Joe Bagley loves plants and could happily live in a jungle. Only one problem. There aren't any jungles in Loughborough, England. So, Joe made one for himself in his apartment. Some people call him *Jungle Boy*.

Joe works in a garden center, so he knows a lot about plants. He has more than 1,400 in his one-bedroom apartment. So far, it's cost him about £3,500 GBP (about $4,200 USD). He also spends a lot of time on his collection, several hours a day. Plants take a lot of care. Joe is so connected to his plant world, he sometimes wakes up in the middle of the night. He knows just which one of his plants needs water or food.

Every available space is packed with flowering plants, tropicals, cacti, succulents, and vines. Even his bathroom is packed with greenery. One plant's vine is so long it snakes around the shower between his shampoo and soaps. It can be hard to get around, but Joe and his dog love their green home.

THUMBS UP IF YOU LOVE PLANTS!

FUN FACT

Joe lives across the street from his grandmother, who thinks he has too many plants. She can't find her way around his apartment. Sometimes Joe smuggles new plants in the back door so she won't see!

Write a response to each question.

1. Why did the author title this passage "Joe's Green Thumb"? Is Joe's thumb actually green?

_____

_____

2. Why did the author say one plant's vine snaked around the shower?

_____

_____

Match each word to its definition.

3. jungle   to take in or out, secretly

4. collection   a place covered with trees, plants, and bushes

5. greenery   green plants

6. smuggle   a group of gathered things that are alike

Solve each problem.

1. If Joe spent $4,200 for all of his 1,400 plants, how much did each plant cost if he spent the same amount on each?

$ _____

2. If Joe buys more plants and now has a total of 1,628 plants, how many did he buy (and sneak by his grandmother)?

_____ plants

3. Joe waters each of his 1,400 plants once a week. How many plants get watered each day?

_____ plants

Complete the table. Answer the question.

4. Joe buys the same number of plants each year.

Year 1	250 plants
Year 2	500 plants
Year 3	750 plants
Year 4	
Year 5	

5. If Joe continued to buy plants in this pattern, during which year would he reach his current total of 1,400 plants?

Year _____

Follow the directions.

Help Joe find his dog! Follow the path of problems whose answers are odd.

START	$3 \times 1 + 4$	$5 \times 3 + 2$	$3 \times 1 + 5$	$4 \times 8 + 2$
$5 \times 3 + 3$	$9 \times 3 + 1$	$6 \times 2 + 1$	$7 \times 8 + 2$	$3 \times 3 + 5$
$9 \times 4 + 2$	$6 \times 2 + 4$	$4 \times 8 + 3$	$9 \times 3 + 2$	$3 \times 6 + 2$
$8 \times 8 + 2$	$5 \times 5 + 5$	$6 \times 6 + 4$	$7 \times 8 + 1$	$4 \times 7 + 2$
$3 \times 2 + 6$	$8 \times 3 + 4$	$2 \times 1 + 4$	$5 \times 1 + 4$	**END**

MEALS FOR MONKEYS

The Monkey Buffet Festival in Lopburi, Thailand, is held to honor the many long-tailed macaque monkeys in the city. These macaques, who number in the thousands, are thought to bring good luck to the people there. So, every November, the city pays them back with a splendid feast.

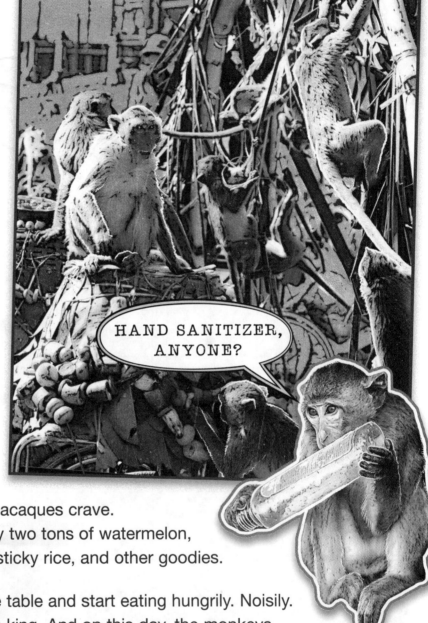

HAND SANITIZER, ANYONE?

The festival opens with a ceremony that includes dancers in monkey costumes. When the macaques show up, sheets are removed from the banquet tables. The table is set with towering pyramids of the colorful fruits and vegetables the macaques crave. The large tables offer nearly two tons of watermelon, durian, lettuce, pineapple, sticky rice, and other goodies.

The macaques jump on the table and start eating hungrily. Noisily. Greedily. It's a feast fit for a king. And on this day, the monkeys are king. But don't worry, off to the side are stands selling food that people can eat!

FUN FACT

Thai legend has it that a monkey king and his army rescued a divine priest's wife after she was kidnapped 2,000 years ago. This festival is a way to show appreciation.

1. What was the author's purpose in writing this text?

_____

_____

2. Adverbs describe an action and often end in *-ly*. Write three adverbs from the text.

_____   _____   _____

3. Find a metaphor the author used to describe the monkeys at this festival.

_____

_____

4. The passages contain mostly facts. What information is not based on fact?

_____

_____

1. The festival has 2,700 pieces of fruit for the monkeys. If each table holds 300 pieces of fruit, how many tables are needed?

_____ tables

2. There are 200 monkeys at the festival. If each monkey eats the same amount of fruit from the tables, about how many pieces of fruit will each monkey eat?

_____ pieces of fruit

3. The festival plans to double the number of tables next year. How many pieces of fruit will they be able to display?

_____ pieces of fruit

4. Last year, the festival used 10 tables for 5 tons of food. About how many pounds of food were on each table? (Hint: 1 ton = 2,000 pounds)

_____ pounds

Write the value of each fruit.

🍌 × 🍌 + 🍌 = 42

(🍍 + 🍉) × 🍌 = 36

🍍 + 🍉 + 🍉 = 8

🍌 × 🍍 × 🍉 = 48

🍌 = _____   🍍 = _____   🍉 = _____

Did you know it's illegal in Alaska to wake a bear to take its photo? This seems bizarre because it is okay to hunt bear in Alaska. It's just not okay to wake them.

In Missouri, it's illegal to drive with a bear that is not in a cage. Who does that? If you live in Oklahoma or Alabama, please don't get into a wrestling match with a bear. If you are caught even trying to train a bear to wrestle, the bear will be taken from you. You also cannot set up a match. You can't let people in. And, you cannot bet money on the outcome.

In South Africa, you may not take a bear with you to a public or private beach. In Memphis, Tennessee, you can't sell teddy bears on a Sunday. There are some real crazy laws on the books. You have to wonder what happened to bring on these laws in the first place.

 **FUN FACT** There don't seem to be any bizarre bear laws in Arizona, but it is against the law to hunt for camels there. You also can't have a donkey in a bathtub after 7 p.m.

Answer each question.

1. Which of the following is not a law mentioned in the text?

   A. No driving with an uncaged bear

   B. No waking bears for photos

   C. No asking bears for directions

   D. No wrestling matches with bears

2. What was the author's purpose in writing this passage?

   A. to inform

   B. to entertain

   C. to persuade

SAY, "HONEY!"

Match each word to its definition.

3. illegal

quite odd or unusual

4. match

against the law

5. bizarre

a contest between two people

Use the table to solve each problem.

Law Broken	Fine
A. Driving with an uncaged bear	$2,415
B. Waking a bear	$328
C. Bringing a bear to the beach	$902
D. Selling a teddy bear on a Sunday	$75
E. Wrestling a bear	$1,864

1. Tyra broke laws C and D. She broke these laws twice. What is her total fine?

   $ _____

2. Wyatt broke laws B and E. He broke these laws three times. What is his total fine?

   $ _____

3. Beau broke laws A, C, and D. He broke law A twice. What is his total fine?

   $ _____

Follow the directions.

Draw four more bears in the grid. No bear should be in the same line (either horizontal, vertical, or diagonal) as another bear.

MAKE A FACE!

Can you make a face that scares people? Do your funny faces put people on the floor laughing? If so, gurning is for you. Gurning means "to pull a grotesque face" in the old English dictionary.

Gurning is a simple sport with few rules. It goes back to 1267. That's more than 750 years ago, but gurning contests are still popular in rural areas of England. So, it's no surprise there is a global competition.

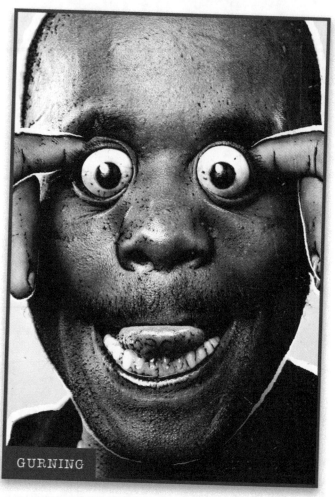

GURNING

The Gurning World Championship is held at the Egremont Crab Apple Fair in northwest England. People come for miles to make faces or watch contestants. Men, women, and even kids can participate. Contestants can't put on makeup and can only wear false teeth if they always do. To compete, they simply stick their heads through a leather horse collar and make their most grotesque faces. Judges decide on a winner.

FUN FACT

No one knows quite how the Gurning World Championship got started, but some think it's because of the face you make if you bite into a sour apple.

Write a response to each question.

1. Which sport is described in this passage? _____

2. Use text evidence to explain the steps for participating in this sport.

_____

_____

_____

3. What is the meaning of *grotesque* as it is used in the text?

_____

Write two antonyms for each word from the text.

4. simple _____

5. rural _____

LIKE THIS?

Complete the table. Use the information to solve each problem.

1. Sally and Simon are professional gurners. Sally charges $12 an hour. Simon charges $11 an hour. How much money would each person earn?

	Sally	Simon
0.5 hour		
1 hour		
1.5 hours		
2 hours		
2.5 hours		
3 hours		

2. How much less does Simon make than Sally for three hours?

$ _____ less

3. How many hours does Sally need to work to earn $54?

_____ hours

4. Simon works for 8 hours each day for four days. How much money will he earn?

$ _____

Make a funny face! Look in a mirror. Draw your face below. Write three words that describe your face.

You probably have favorite Olympic sports. Gymnastics? Swimming? Figure skating? Snowboarding? Those are very popular, year after year. They'll probably be Olympic sports for a long time. What about art, music, and poetry? They're not sports, but they once were Olympic events.

The modern Olympic Games began in 1896. In addition to sports, the Olympics awarded medals for painting, sculpture, architecture, literature, and music. Although the fine art competition was enjoyed, it was still not as popular as the sporting events.

Olympic events continue to fall in and out of popularity. Some events are no longer part of the games. Motorboating was once an event. People were bored. Polo ran for only five seasons. It was fun, but it was expensive and complicated. Track-and-field events included tug-of-war for centuries. Other events that have disappeared from the Olympic lineup include croquet, ballooning, roller hockey, and bowling. Which events would you like to see come back?

FUN FACT

One of the more unusual Olympic sports that has disappeared is glima. It is a type of wrestling in which you can only use the other person's belt to throw them to the ground.

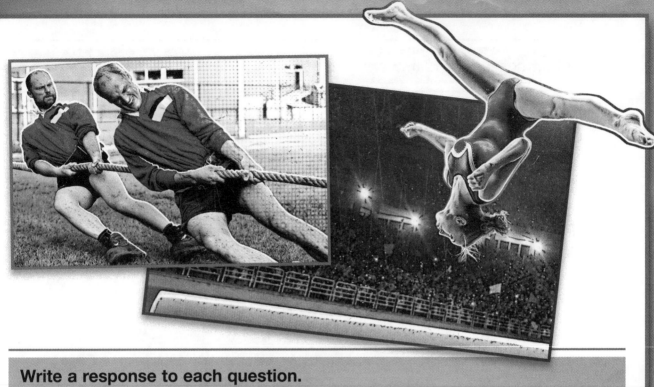

Write a response to each question.

1. What is the main idea of this text?

_____

_____

2. What is your favorite Olympic sport today? Explain.

_____

_____

Write a homophone from the text for each word.

(Hint: Homophones are words that sound the same but are spelled differently.)

3. four _____

4. board _____

5. there _____

Use the infographic to answer each question.

Olympic Games by the Numbers

water bottles	5,000,000
toilet flushes	1,250,000
bags of trash	336,000
meals	45,000
pillows	22,000
medals	4,700

1. Which object was used $1.25 \times 1,000,000$ times?

   _____

2. Which object was given out $4.7 \times 1,000$ times?

   _____

3. These were provided $4.5 \times 10,000$ times.

   _____

4. These were filled $3.36 \times 100,000$ times.

   _____

Follow the directions.

Let's play croquet! The mallet whacks the ball through the wickets. The ball follows a path through numbers that when added equal 10,000. Draw the path.

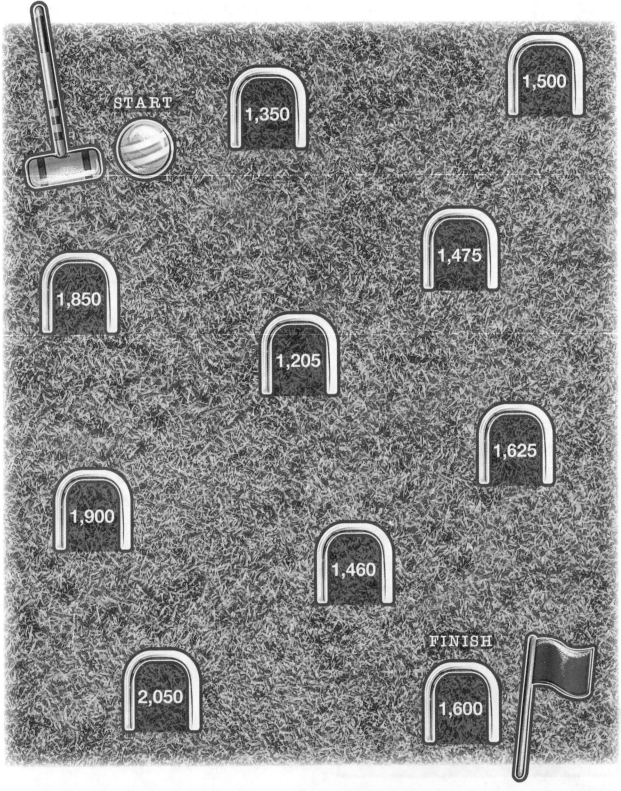

COOL HAIR!

Have you ever heard of a hair-freezing contest? It's strange but true. The Takhini Hot Springs Hair Freezing Contest is an annual winter event near Whitehorse, Yukon. That's a Canadian territory.

The hot spring is toasty at 47°C (116°F). It's the outside air that's cold in winter months. So, when the outside temperature drops below -20°C (-6°F), it's hair-freezing time.

FUN FACT

The grand prize of the Hair Freezing Contest is $2,000 Canadian dollars (about $1,535 USD) and unlimited soaks in the hot springs.

Follow three steps to win a hair-freezing contest. First, dip all the way under the hot water. Then, poke your head out and wait for your hair to freeze. Your eyelashes and eyebrows will also freeze. Don't let your ears freeze! Dip them in the hot spring to keep them from freezing too.

As your hair freezes, make it stylish! Pat in waves and curls or fashion a headful of spikes. Once your hair is white, frosty, and fashionable, you're ready. Ring the bell to get a photo taken of your icy masterpiece. May the best ice head win!

Answer the question.

1. Which of these statements tell what the passage is mostly about?

   A. It is really cold in Whitehorse, Yukon.

   B. A hair-freezing contest is held in Whitehorse, Yukon.

   C. There are hot springs in Whitehorse, Yukon.

Write a response to each question.

2. Write the three steps to winning a hair-freezing contest.

   _____

   _____

   _____

3. Write a different title for this passage.

   _____

4. Would you like to enter a hair-freezing contest? Explain.

   _____

1. How many degrees difference is there between the temperature in the water versus the temperature of the air? (In degrees Celsius)

_____ degrees

2. How many degrees difference is there between the temperature in the water versus the temperature of the air? (In degrees Fahrenheit)

_____ degrees

3. If you won the contest every year for four years, how much money would you earn in Canadian dollars? In US dollars?

$ _____ CAD $ _____ USD

Follow the directions.

Draw a winning frozen hair style. Measure the height and width of your final style. Write the measurements in inches or centimeters.

Height: _____   Width: _____

GUINEA PIG BFFS

Guinea pigs are much like you and me. They want friends. They are quite social creatures. Before they were tamed, they lived in herds of 10 or more. They play, snuggle, and communicate with one another.

Many people keep guinea pigs as pets. They're small and easy to raise. But, guinea pigs don't do so well by themselves. They get lonely and depressed. They may even get sick or develop behavior problems. A human is not enough. They need a furry friend of their own.

For this reason, the European country of Switzerland made it illegal in 2008 to keep only one guinea pig. The Swiss government believes in certain animal rights. They consider it cruel to keep just one guinea pig at a time. At first, some people thought it was a silly law. Then, more and more people realized that lonely guinea pigs were suffering. Guinea pigs need friendship just like the rest of us. So, if you've got a guinea pig, make sure it's got lots of company.

FUN FACT

In Switzerland, you can rent a guinea pig! For a small fee, guinea pig owners can take home a new buddy to comfort a grieving pet whose companion died.

WE'RE DEFINITELY CLOSE FRIENDS.

Answer each question.

1. What does **not** happen when guinea pigs are left alone?

   A. They eat too much.

   B. They get lonely and depressed.

   C. They may get sick.

   D. They may develop behavior problems.

2. Why does the author think people keep guinea pigs as pets?

   A. They do not eat a lot.

   B. They don't have to be taken on walks.

   C. They are small and easy to raise.

   D. They are quiet at night.

DON'T WORRY. I'VE GOT YOUR BACK.

Write a response to each question.

3. Why is it illegal in Switzerland to have only one guinea pig?

   _____

   _____

4. Do you think the author agrees with this law? Support your answer with evidence from the text.

   _____

   _____

Use >, <, or = to compare the numbers in each problem.

1. Greta's Guinea Pigs loaned 6,524 guinea pigs last year. This year she loaned 6,542 guinea pigs.

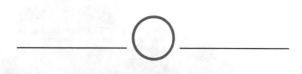

2. Peter's Pets sold 8,990 guinea pigs since it opened. Greta's Guinea Pigs sold 8,890 guinea pigs since it opened.

Answer each question.

3. You see 56 guinea pig legs under the pen's walls. How many guinea pigs are in the pen?

224 guinea pigs   56 guinea pigs   14 guinea pigs

4. You see 12 guinea pig legs under one pen's walls. You see 36 guinea pig legs under another pen's walls. How many guinea pigs are in the pens? Which equation does **not** show how to solve this problem?

$(12 + 36) \div 4$ $12 \div 4 + 36 \div 4$ $12 + 36 \div 4$

Follow the directions.

Greta's Guinea Pigs needs to build new pens that hold two guinea pigs. Each guinea pig needs a space that is 8 square feet. Design at least two new pens for Greta's Guinea Pigs.

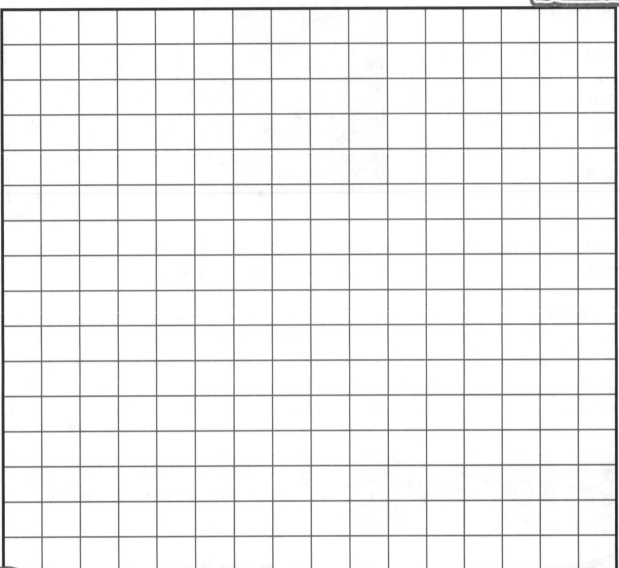

1 square unit = 1 square foot

What is the area of each new pen? _____

What is the shortest perimeter of the two designs? _____

COLORFUL UNDIES

It is hard to believe that the color of your underwear means anything. But some people believe it does.

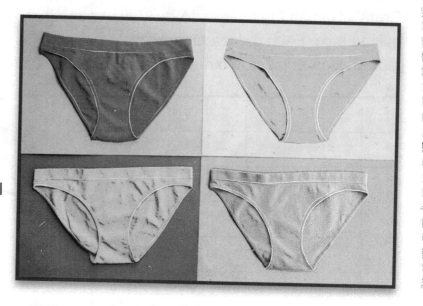

If it's New Year's Day, try wearing yellow underpants! Some people believe this will bring you riches in the new year. This custom is popular mostly in places where people speak Spanish, such as Spain, Mexico, and some countries in South America. The rules for lucky underwear vary. Some people believe yellow underwear is only lucky if it was received as a gift.

These are just superstitions. But just in case, don't throw away the other colors in your drawer. There are more underwear superstitions. Wear white when life is stressful, and you need peace. Put on black undies to feel strong and reach goals. Green underwear will send an adventure your way. And, blue undies will put you in the mood for healthy food and exercise. It's all about dressing for what you want.

FUN FACT You can also give yourself a lucky day with any color of underwear. Just wear them inside out!

ONE LUCKY GIFT!

Write a response to each question.

1. Use context clues to explain what the word *superstition* means.

   _____

   _____

2. Do you think the author believes the color of underwear can be lucky? Use text evidence to support your answer.

   _____

   _____

3. Tell about a superstition you or someone you know believes in.

   _____

   _____

Write an antonym for each word from the text.

4. stressful _____

5. believe _____

6. healthy _____

Graph the data. Round each number to the nearest hundred.

At the New Year's Day parade, attendees were asked what color of underwear they are wearing. The survey results are below.

Underwear Color	
Red	250
Orange	410
Yellow	1,010
Green	210
Blue	320
Purple	130
White	670
Black	550

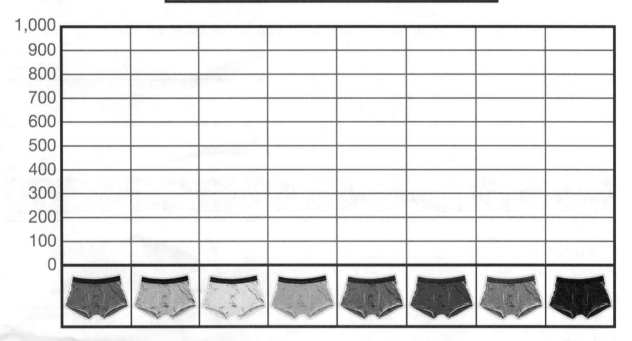

1. Which color underwear was the least worn at the parade? _____

2. Which two colors were worn by about the same number of people?

_____ _____

3. About how many people attended the parade? _____ people

1. Draw different ways you can arrange three underwear on a clothesline.

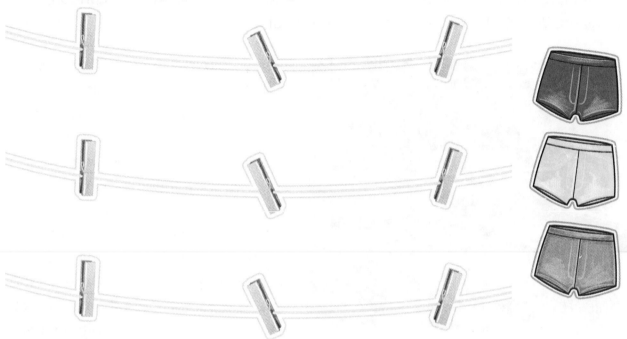

2. Draw different ways you can arrange four underwear on a clothesline.

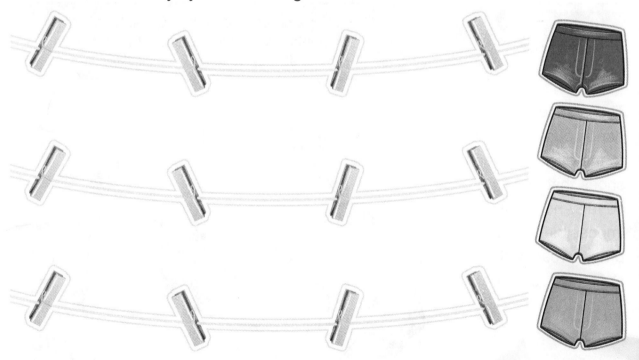

ILLEGAL SHOES

In 1463, during the Middle Ages, long-toed shoes were outlawed in London, England. What? Who cares about the length of a shoe?

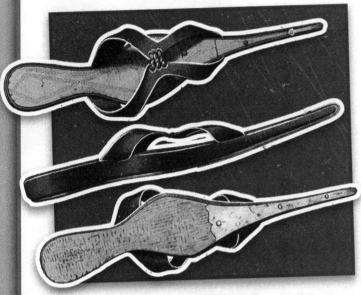

Rich, young lords cared. They wanted to show off. They wore ridiculous shoes called *crakows* or *poulaines*. The shoes were expensive and told people the lord was wealthy. Crakows were funny-looking, shaped like carrots. They often stuck out as much as five inches (13 cm) past the big toe. The longest point ever on a crakow measured 20 inches (50 cm). The points made them look like elves' shoes. They were often stuffed so they wouldn't curl too much or flop over. Sometimes the points were fastened by gold or silver chains to a bracelet around the leg!

FUN FACT

For a short time in the 1950s, long-toed, pointy shoes came back in fashion. This time they were called *winklepickers*.

These shoes were dangerous! It was easy to trip over feet wearing shoes that stuck out so far. And, it was impossible to kneel in prayer wearing these shoes. So, they were banned.

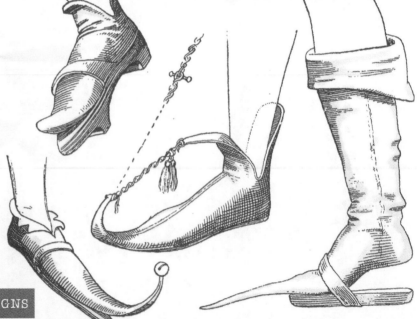

EARLY POULAINE DESIGNS

_____ **1.** Long-toed shoes were once worn by wealthy lords.

_____ **2.** The lords wore them to defend themselves.

_____ **3.** Some shoes had to be stuffed so they didn't flop over.

_____ **4.** These long shoes were fastened with belts.

Write a response to each question.

5. Find the simile in this passage. What two things are compared?

_____

_____

6. If you were in charge, would you let people wear long-toed shoes? Explain.

_____

_____

A GIFT OF BETTER SHOES

TOTALLY ILLEGAL

Measure each shoe in centimeters. Write the lengths.

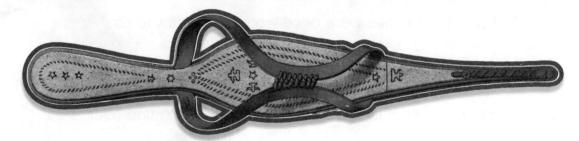

1. _____ cm

2. _____ cm

3. _____ cm

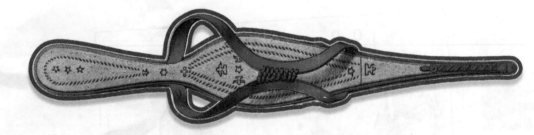

4. _____ cm

Follow the directions.

There are so many different shoes! Find 12 shoe styles hidden in the puzzle.

BOOT	SANDAL	MUKLUK
STILETTO	LOAFER	MOCCASIN
WEDGE	SNEAKER	SLIPPER
MOJARI	ESPADRILLE	OKOBO

```
A  H  M  I  U  L  O  A  F  E  R  U  K  M
H  K  G  D  B  A  D  H  K  J  H  R  D  N
G  L  H  T  T  D  B  X  C  S  R  F  G  W
T  Q  Y  T  H  D  M  N  W  S  A  J  L
M  A  O  V  R  A  I  U  V  E  C  I  O  P
M  O  C  C  A  S  I  N  L  A  D  X  P  V
B  T  K  S  Q  W  V  L  B  K  D  G  B  Z
U  T  Y  O  E  R  I  Z  V  E  D  P  E  S
K  E  U  O  B  R  P  M  F  R  J  K  J  L
G  L  S  S  D  O  U  Y  P  T  U  I  A  I
R  I  J  A  K  B  D  R  Y  L  J  K  D  P
B  T  P  O  T  Y  T  D  K  N  R  R  H  P
N  S  N  G  A  S  D  U  H  T  Y  M  N  E
E  O  Z  F  S  P  M  O  J  A  R  I  O  R
```

What do people do if they want to buy a house today? Call a real estate agent! Then, they drive around looking at all the houses for sale. Once, there were other choices.

In the first half of the 20th century, you could buy a house from a store! Sears, Roebuck, and Company sold them in their mail-order catalog. Today, it would be like buying a home from Amazon. Who does that? As many as 75,000 people did! The first Sears catalog of homes offered 44 styles in prices ranging from $360 to $2,890. That was a lot of money back then. The first mail-order home sold in 1908.

FUN FACT

One year, Sears sold a two-story schoolhouse with six classrooms, a library, an auditorium, and an office. It cost $11,500.

AN ORIGINAL SEARS KIT HOME
STILL STANDING TODAY

The homes were sold as kits. They had everything needed to build a house. The kits were shipped on railroad boxcars. Family, friends, and neighbors helped the new homeowners put the house together. Sometimes, they hired carpenters and electricians to help. Some of the mail-order homes are still standing, but they are hard to identify. Records were lost.

1. What was the author's purpose in writing this passage?

   A. to inform

   B. to entertain

   C. to persuade

2. Which statement is **not** true about the house kits?

   A. The kits contained everything needed to build a house.

   B. Family, friends, and neighbors helped put the house together.

   C. The houses were delivered on big trucks.

   D. The kits were shipped by railroad.

Write a response to the question.

3. If you could buy a house kit today, what features would you want? Write 3–5 sentences describing the kit.

   _____

   _____

   _____

   _____

   _____

   _____

Solve each problem.

1. The Mabe family wants to buy a house kit for $1,320. If the family saves $40 a month, how many months will they need to save to buy the kit?

_____ months

2. The Smith family wants to buy a house kit for $624. If the family saves $12 a week, how many weeks will they need to save to buy the kit? About how many months is that?

_____ weeks   _____ months

3. New Town wants to purchase a school kit for $10,800. Last year the town raised $4,930. How much more do they need to raise to buy the school kit?

$ _____

4. Acme Builders wants to buy 12 house kits for their housing development. If each kit costs $410, how much will they spend on kits?

$ _____

5. The Johnson family saved some money to buy a kit. They need to save $128 more to buy the $1,150 kit. How much have they saved so far?

$ _____

Draw the missing houses so that each color of house appears only once in each row, column, or square.

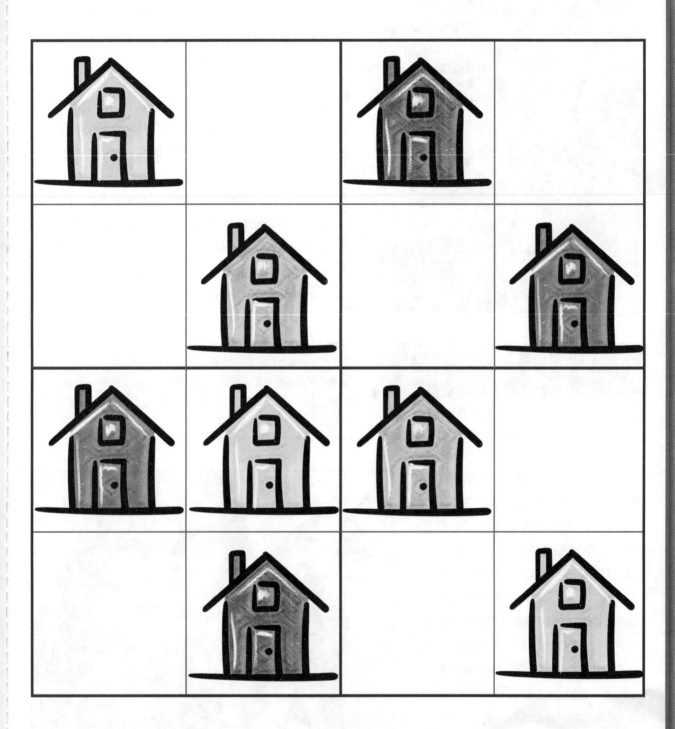

Ancient Egyptians cared a lot about how they looked. They worked at it. Both men and women wore makeup. To be beautiful was to be holy, to give praise to their gods. They also believed makeup was good for their skin and their self-confidence.

Lipstick and eye shadow were widely used. Green eye shadow was most popular. It was made from grinding a stone called *malachite*. The most common makeup was black eyeliner, called *kohl*. It was made by grinding the mineral galena. Besides making a person look good, kohl was thought to protect the eyes from the desert sun.

FUN FACT

The ancient Egyptian queen, Cleopatra, was known to wear a special lipstick made from flowers, red ochre, fish scales, crushed bugs, and beeswax.

The ancient Egyptians had many interesting body care rituals. Almond oil was used to condition hair. A lotion made with milk and honey kept the skin soft. They scrubbed all over with sea salt. If they had unwanted body hair, they plucked it out with tweezers made from seashells. It took a lot of work to be holy!

Write a response to each question.

1. What is the main idea of the passage?

____

____

2. Identify two key details that support the main idea.

____

____

____

____

Match each word to its definition.

3. malachite	black eyeliner
4. kohl	a dark gray mineral
5. galena	a bright green stone

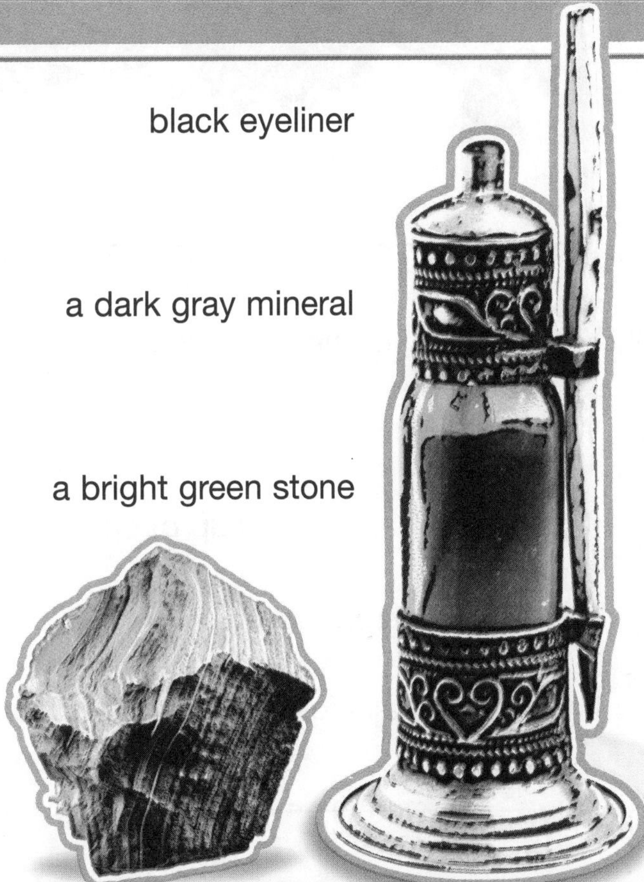

CLEOPATRA'S FAVORITE LIPSTICK

1 PART ORCHID

2 PARTS RED OCHRE

3 PARTS FISH SCALES

2 PARTS CRUSHED BEETLES

4 PARTS BEESWAX

1. What fraction of the recipe is fish scales? _____

2. What fraction of the recipe is ochre? _____

3. What fraction of the recipe is orchid and beetles? _____

4. If the recipe calls for $\frac{1}{2}$ cup of ochre, how much beeswax would you need?

    _____

5. If the recipe calls for 8 cups of beeswax, how much orchid would you need?

    _____

Follow the directions.

Find the names of 10 ancient beauty ingredients hidden in the puzzle.

MALACHITE	MILK	FISH SCALES
GALENA	SALT	KOHL
HONEY	BEESWAX	CRUSHED BUGS
	OCHRE	

C S J R L G S A L T B E O G
B R T N F N O F G H T L A X
M N U Y I C V H I I J K A P
S H G S S N K O H L L W X Z
M B O I H K Z C P O S B D O
I A S D S E A U I E L K F C
L V B N C L D I E J P H O H
K F R H A J H B K L L O B R
C V B M L K J H U U T N J E
V G A L E N A K M G D E E N
A S D F S J W E R O S Y P Q
C V B J F T Y P I R E Q Z N

SUPER SNEEZE

When you drive on a country road, you are probably going 35 miles an hour (56 km/h). That's slow. You can speed along a six-lane highway at about 70 miles an hour (113 km/h). That's fast!

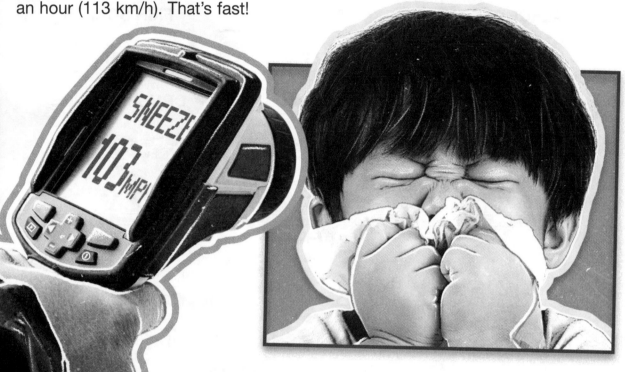

Do you know what is even faster? A sneeze! The fastest sneeze ever measured blew out at 103 miles per hour (166 km/h). Couldn't you get a ticket for that? When you sneeze, the back part of your throat is cut off. All that air is forced out through your nose at once. Achoo!

When you cough, the back of your throat is not closed off. But, the chest pressure is still powerful. Hearty coughs have been measured between 60 and 70 miles per hour (97 and 113 km/h). Still, that's a speed for a six-lane highway.

Finally, let's talk about burping. Most burps come from swallowing too much air. When there is too much air at the stomach opening, it comes up and out. Burps escape as fast as 60 to 70 miles per hour (97 to 113 km/h). A burp is as fast as a cough. Who knew?

 **FUN FACT** How fast does a fart travel? Seven miles per hour (11.3 km/h)!

Write a response to each question.

1. When you read the title, what did you think the passage would be about?

_____

_____

2. Write two things that surprised you in this passage.

_____

_____

3. What four body noises are mentioned in this passage?

_____

_____

_____

_____

Match each action with its speed.

4. sneeze   60–70 miles per hour (97–113 km/h)

5. cough   103 miles per hour (166 km/h)

6. fart   7 miles per hour (11.3 km/h)

Solve each problem.

1. Dani's sneeze is 46 mph. Her brother's sneeze is twice as fast. How fast is her brother's sneeze?

_____ mph

2. Brady's cough is 96 km/h. His dad's sneeze is half as fast. How fast is his dad's sneeze?

_____ km/h

Answer each question.

3. Kaden's burp is 61 mph. Austin's burp is 23 mph slower. Which expression shows how to solve for the speed of Austin's burp?

$61 + 23$ $61 - 23$ 61×23

4. Bridget's sneeze is slow at 43 km/h. Her mom's sneeze is three times faster. Which equation does **not** show how to solve for the speed of her mom's sneeze?

3×43 $43 + 3$ $43 + 43 + 43$

Follow the directions.

It's sneeze season! You have some boxes of tissues to place on the store shelves. Read the clues and draw the boxes on display. Answer the question.

- There are three shelves.

- You cannot put the same amount of boxes on each shelf.

- You must put an even number of boxes on each shelf.

Question: What's the least number of boxes you must have?

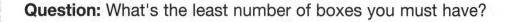

Answer: _____ boxes

In 2010, a 75-year-old Massachusetts man was rushed to the hospital. Ron Sveden could hardly breathe. He worried he had a tumor growing in his lungs.

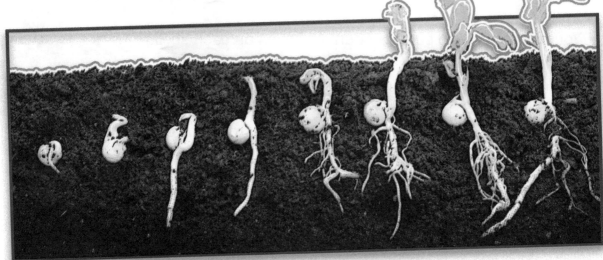

An X-ray showed it was not a tumor. It was a pea plant! Yes, it was the kind of pea plant that usually grows in a garden. Everyone was flabbergasted. How did it get there? They finally guessed that a pea Ron ate must have gone down his throat into his lungs instead of his stomach. The pea seed split and sprouted.

FUN FACT

A dandelion was removed from a 16-month-old baby's ear after a 4-month earache. The plant was nearly an inch (2 cm) long and had to be surgically removed.

Plants need moisture, warmth, and sunlight to grow. A lung has both moisture and warmth. There is no sunlight, but seeds can sprout underground. The sprout was only a half inch (1.3 cm) long, but it was still growing. A surgeon removed the small plant. Ron went home and recovered. And, he continued to eat his peas!

NOT FOR THE PEA!

WHAT A HAP-PEA ENDING!

Answer each question.

1. Why was Ron Sveden rushed to the hospital in 2010?

    A. He had a lung disease.

    B. He could hardly breathe.

    C. He was having a heart attack.

2. What did an X-ray show?

    A. It showed a tumor in his chest.

    B. It showed a hole in his lung.

    C. It showed a pea plant growing in his lung.

Write a response to each question.

3. Write three things a plant needs to grow. Circle the two that Ron's lung had.

    _____   _____   _____

4. Name another plant that grew inside someone's body. Include two details.

_____

_____

_____

Use the table to answer each question.

Plant Growth

Day	Height in Inches
1	0.25
2	0.50
3	1
4	2

1. If a pea plant continues to grow in the same pattern, about how many inches tall will it be on day 6?

   _____ in.

2. If a pea plant continues to grow in the same pattern, on what day would it reach 16 inches?

   Day _____

3. If a pea plant continues to grow in the same pattern, about how many inches tall will it be on day 9?

   _____ in.

4. If a pea plant continues to grow in the same pattern, on what day would it reach 128 inches?

   Day _____

Use the code to reveal the fun fact.

1	2	3	4	5	6	7	8	9	10	11	12	13
A	B	C	D	E	F	G	H	I	J	K	L	M

14	15	16	17	18	19	20	21	22	23	24	25	26
N	O	P	Q	R	S	T	U	V	W	X	Y	Z

A similar case as Ron's occurred in 2009. A Russian man had this type of plant growing inside his lung. He also made a full recovery.

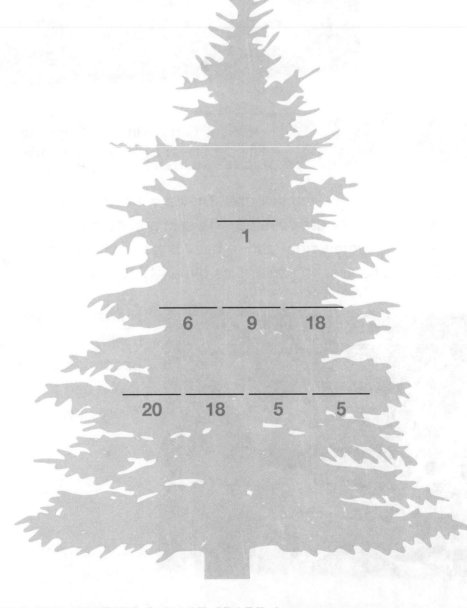

$\overline{}$
1

$\overline{}$ $\overline{}$ $\overline{}$
6   9   18

$\overline{}$ $\overline{}$ $\overline{}$ $\overline{}$
20   18   5   5

NOT A FAIRY "TAIL"

It may be hard to believe, but most humans have a tail while in their mother's body. It usually disappears within eight weeks. It grows into the tailbone. Sometimes, the tail does not disappear. Instead, the human baby is born with a tail. It is called a *vestigial tail* and is very rare.

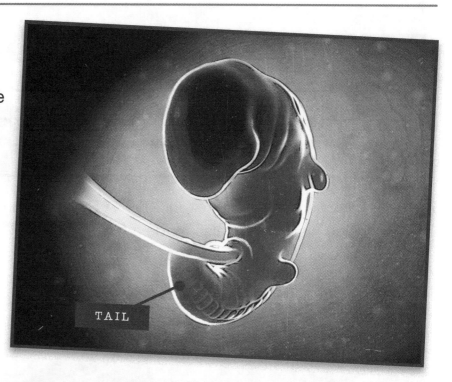

TAIL

FUN FACT

In some parts of India, a human tail is thought to be a gift from the gods.

The tails are always located on the tailbone. They are made of muscle, blood vessels, fat, and nerves. They are covered with skin and do not contain bone. Most are removed with surgery right after a baby is born. Others may keep their tails for years. Doctors have seen patients as old as 17 who still have their tails.

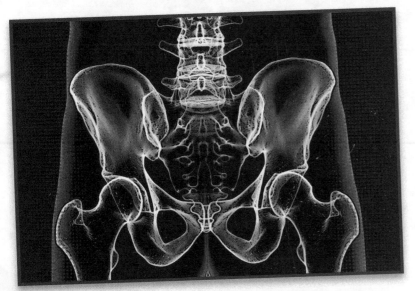

Human tails are not a health problem but can be uncomfortable. Imagine if you had to sit on a tail every day!

Write a response to each question.

1. Explain why the author put quotation marks around "Tail" in the title.

_____

_____

_____

2. Write the sentence from the text that tells the author's opinion.

_____

_____

3. Would you rather have a tail like a monkey or a tail like a horse? Explain.

_____

_____

Circle the part of speech of each word from the text.

4. rare   noun   verb   adjective

5. problem   noun   verb   adjective

6. disappear   noun   verb   adjective

7. uncomfortable   noun   verb   adjective

8. human   noun   verb   adjective

Measure each tail to the nearest quarter inch. Write the lengths.

1.

_____ in.

2.

_____ in.

3.

_____ in.

4.

_____ in.

5.

_____ in.

Solve the problems to find the answer to each question.

1. **Question**: What has a head and a tail but no body?

314	874	882	307	686
+562	+893	+999	+692	+734
= I	= N	= O	= A	= C

Answer: ____ ____ ____ ____ ____
999 1,420 1,881 876 1,767

"TAIL" ME MORE JOKES!

2. **Question**: Where do lizards go when their tails come off?

5,123	5,506	2,376	2,053
+3,011	+2,002	+1,484	+8,761
= A	= T	= L	= R

3,212	4,909
+3,391	+2,080
= E	= I

Answer: The ____ ____ ____ ____ ____ ____ Store
10,814 6,603 7,508 8,134 6,989 3,860

PRUNEY FINGERS

Did you ever notice that your fingers look like prunes after you've had your hands in water for a long time? Check your fingers the next time you're in a pool or have had a long bath. Are they wrinkled?

Don't worry. That pruney look is normal. When your hands are in water, your nervous system sends a message to the blood vessels in your fingers. It tells them to shrink. When the blood vessels shrink, the skin is not as tight. It wrinkles. But the wrinkles will go away.

No one knows for sure why this happens. Scientists think that it's so your fingers can grip things better when they are wet. Toes also wrinkle in water. Maybe that's to help you run or walk better when your feet are wet.

Mild pruning can also happen if you don't drink enough. Children your age should drink at least five cups of beverages a day, including milk and water.

FUN FACT

Here's a fun fact about the word *prunes*. Photographers in the 19th century had people say "prunes" because it kept their mouths prim, or proper. Do you wonder why we say "cheese" nowadays? To keep your mouth in a smile!

Write a response to each question.

1. Find the simile in this passage. What two things are compared?

_____

_____

2. What happens to your fingers when your hands are in water?

_____

_____

_____

3. What do you think the author wants you to remember from this text?

_____

_____

Write two synonyms for each word from the text.

4. grip _____

5. normal _____

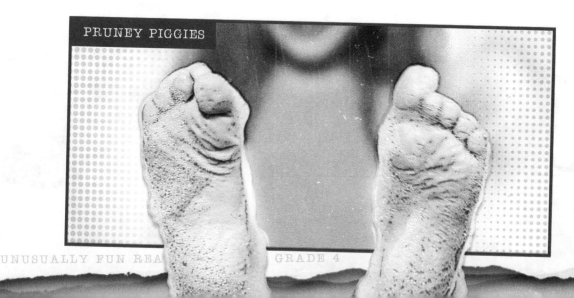

PRUNEY PIGGIES

Follow the directions.

Draw a line to match each mixed number to its equivalent improper fraction. To solve the riddle, write the letters in order on the lines.

Question: What gets wetter the more it dries?

1. $4\frac{7}{8}$　　　　　　　　　　　　　　　　　$\frac{17}{8}$　O

2. $1\frac{1}{2}$　　　　　　　　　　　　　　　　　$\frac{7}{2}$　L

3. $2\frac{1}{8}$　　　　　　　　　　　　　　　　　$\frac{39}{7}$　E

4. $3\frac{2}{3}$　　　　　　　　　　　　　　　　　$\frac{3}{2}$　T

5. $5\frac{4}{7}$　　　　　　　　　　　　　　　　　$\frac{39}{8}$　A

6. $3\frac{1}{2}$　　　　　　　　　　　　　　　　　$\frac{11}{3}$　W

Answer:

_____

____ ____ ____ ____ ____

Connect the dots from least to greatest to reveal a common victim of pruney skin. Begin at the star.

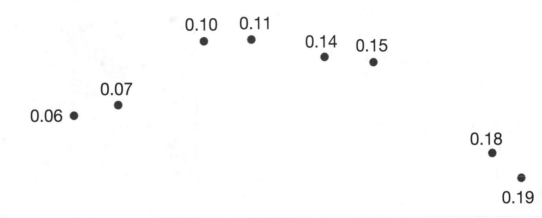

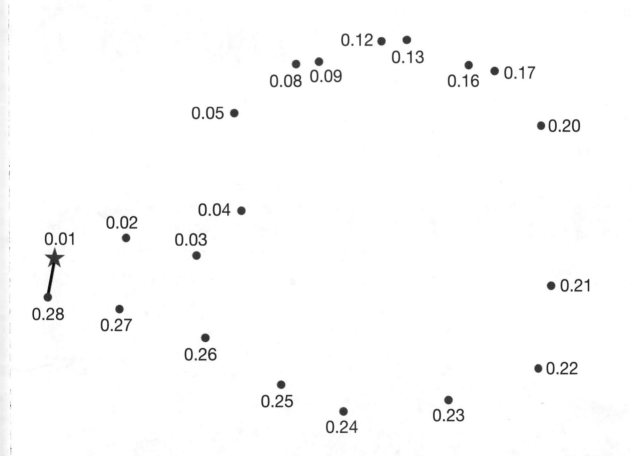

It's amazing but true. You shed about 500 million flakes of skin every single day. Look at that huge number: 500,000,000. You shed your entire layer of skin every two to four weeks. It's amazing you have any skin left. Don't worry. You have about 300 trillion skin cells in all. That's a three with 14 zeros behind it!

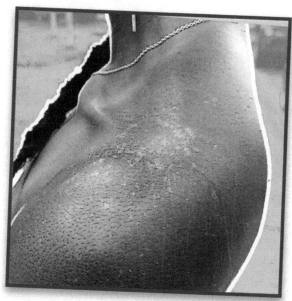

These numbers change depending on who you talk to. But scientists have made a good study of our flaking bodies. One way to get a good count is to put a cup over a patch of skin for a day. Then, they can weigh the skin cells that have fallen into the cup. Try it!

Here's another big number: 12 million. That's about how many skin cells flake off in your bed while you're sleeping. The bad news is that dust mites love to eat dead skin cells. That's why up to 10 million dust mites are probably in your bed!

FUN FACT

Dust mites are tiny bugs you'll never see. They have eight legs and no wings. They are mostly harmless, but they can cause allergies.

I ♥ skin flakes

Answer each question.

1. How many flakes of skin do you shed every day?

   A. 2 trillion   B. 500 million   C. 500 billion

2. How often do you shed your entire layer of skin?

   A. every two to four weeks

   B. once a month

   C. twice a year

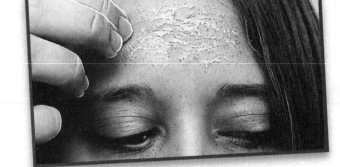

3. What is a dust mite?

   A. a kind of spider

   B. a tiny bug that eats skin cells found in dust

   C. a tool used to clean furniture

Write two different meanings for each word from the passage.

---

4. shed

_____

_____

5. change

_____

_____

Solve each problem.

1. If you shed 500 million skin cells every day, how many skin cells would you shed after 2 days?

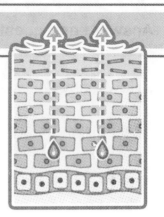

_____ skin cells

2. If you shed 500 million skin cells every day, how many skin cells would you shed after 4 days?

_____ skin cells

Use the information above to complete the table.

(The first row has been done for you.)

Total Skin Cells Lost	
Day 1	500,000,000
Day 2	
Day 3	
Day 4	
Day 5	
Day 6	
Day 7	

1. This is the largest three-digit number you can make using different digits.

   _____ _____ _____

2. This is the smallest four-digit number you can make using different digits.

   _____ , _____ _____ _____

3. This five-digit number has all odd digits that are in order from least to greatest.

   _____ _____ , _____ _____ _____

4. This is the sum of the smallest four-digit number and the largest three-digit number.

   _____ , _____ _____ _____

You probably don't think much about your nails because you've always had them. You had them even before you were born. Nails are important. They have jobs to do. They protect the tender tips of our fingers. They help us pick up small things. And, they can be fun to paint!

FUN FACT

A Utah woman, Lee Redmond, did not cut her nails for 29 years. Her right thumbnail was nearly three feet (1 m) long!

Nails are made of keratin. Keratin is a type of protein your body makes. It is also found in your hair and on your skin. Keratin hardens cells that grow from the nail root under the cuticle. A nail forms from the old cells that new cells push out. The nail grows and slides along the nail bed.

Fingernails grow slowly. It takes three to six months to grow a new nail. That seems like a long time. But, replacing a toenail can take a year or a year and a half. That's three times as long as it takes to regrow a fingernail. Fingernails grow faster in the summer than in the winter. No one knows why for sure, but it may be because there's more sunlight. Sunshine creates more Vitamin D.

Take care of your nails. About 20 to 30 percent of people bite their nails. Do you? Try to quit. First, germs collect under fingernails. Also, nails should look nice. Long ago in China, people knew how important you were by how long and beautiful your nails were.

Write a response to each question.

1. What does the author mean by saying nails "have jobs to do"?

_____

_____

2. Why does the author think you should not bite your nails?

_____

_____

Answer each question.

3. Which sentence is an opinion?

A. Fingernails help us pick up small things.

B. Fingernails are fun to paint.

C. Fingernails protect your fingertips.

4. Which is **not** true about Lee Redmond?

A. She did not cut her nails for 29 years.

B. She is from Utah.

C. She constantly bit her nails.

D. Her right thumbnail was nearly three feet (1 m) long.

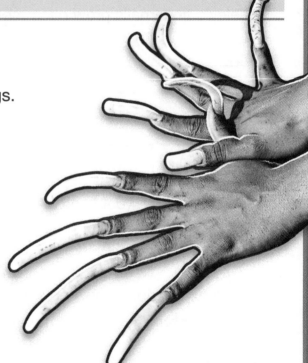

Solve each problem.

1. Ruby and Reagan want to grow long fingernails. Ruby's nails grow $\frac{1}{8}$ of an inch each month. Reagan's nails grow $\frac{1}{10}$ of an inch each month. Whose nails will grow 1 inch long first? Explain.

_____

_____

2. How many months would it take?

_____ months

3. Neeley's fingernails grow twice as fast as Reagan's fingernails. How much do Neeley's fingernails grow each month?

_____ in.

Answer each question.

4. Lee Redmond's thumbnail grew to 1 meter long in 29 years. Which expression shows how you would solve for how many centimeters it grew each year?

$29 \div 1 \times 100$ $100 \div 29$ $100 - 29$

5. Which expression shows how you would solve for how many centimeters Lee's thumbnail grew each month?

$100 \div (29 \times 12) = ?$ $29 \div (100 \times 12) = ?$ $12 \div (29 \times 100) = ?$

Follow the directions.

Would you believe that it is someone's job to name the different colors of nail polish? Be creative! Name each color. The first one is done for you.

 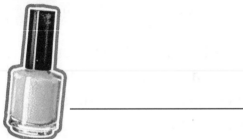 _Strawberry Jam_

 _____

 _____

 _____

 _____

 _____

"Paint" these nails for fun. Add designs.

PIG OUT!

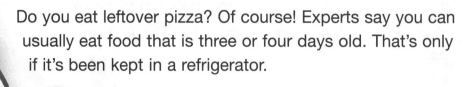

Do you eat leftover pizza? Of course! Experts say you can usually eat food that is three or four days old. That's only if it's been kept in a refrigerator.

But what about a 120-year-old ham? Yes, there's a piece of pork with that many birthdays. It sports a gold collar and was once someone's pet ham. After being lost for 20 years, it was found and kept in an iron safe. It was taken out every day to show it off.

This old ham has not rotted because it was cured. People have been curing meat for centuries. Today, most curing is done with combinations of salt, sugar, and other things to dry out the meat.

FUN FACT

Sitting about five feet away from the world's oldest ham is the world's oldest peanut. The peanut is still in its shell, with the date *1890* written on it.

Some think this old piece of ham could be eaten, but no one wants to try it! It would be like chewing on a leather shoe. And, it is not on the menu! It is on display at a Virginia museum. It has a Twitter account and can be watched live on the museum's *HAM CAM*.

Write a response to each question.

1. Name two things on display at a Virginia museum.

2. Would you eat a chunk of this old ham? Explain.

Write two different meanings for each word from the passage.

3. safe

4. sports

5. cured

1. Rover's favorite Saturday activity is watching the HAM CAM. He started watching it at 2:30 p.m. If he watched it for 1 hour 35 minutes, what time did he stop?

_____ p.m.

2. Lady watched the HAM CAM from 11:15 a.m. to 12:45 p.m. How long did Lady watch the HAM CAM?

_____ hours or _____ hour, _____ minutes

3. Binky and Dinky stopped watching the Ham Cam at 6:05 p.m. They watched for a total of 2 hours and 10 minutes. What time did Binky and Dinky start watching the HAM CAM?

_____ p.m.

4. Fluff and Nutter both watched the same amount of HAM CAM yesterday. Fluff started at 10:30 a.m. and stopped at 2:55 p.m. Nutter started at 9:20 a.m. What time did he stop watching the HAM CAM?

_____ p.m.

The year that each food item was purchased is on each label. Write how old each food item is based on the current year.

1. apples _____

2. eggs _____

3. lettuce _____

4. cheese _____

5. cookies _____

6. fried chicken _____

OUT OF MY LANE!

Have you noticed the white lines on highways? Whoever is driving the car pays attention to them. Maybe you've even noticed them in video games you play.

These lines divide two or more lanes of traffic. Sometimes there are white and yellow lines. It's important for cars to stay in their own lanes. The lines can be solid or dashed. Solid lines mean you can't pass the car in front of you even if it's just poking along. The dashed lines mean that you can pass if no other car is in the other lane.

FUN FACT

Take a quick look at a dashed line when driving. How long do you think each dash is? A couple feet? Think again. They are 10 feet (3 m) long!

Roads weren't always marked this way. But in 1911, a Michigan road supervisor named Edward Hines noticed a milk wagon leaking a line of milk on the road. It gave him an idea. By 1917, painted center lines were the law in Michigan, California, and Oregon.

Complete each sentence with a word from the word bank.

dashed	highways	lanes	solid

1. Most _____ have lines dividing them into two or

 more _____.

2. Some of the lines are _____, meaning you can't pass.

3. Other lines are _____, meaning you can pass if it's safe.

Write a response to each question.

4. What was Edward Hines's big idea and what was the result?

 _____

 _____

 _____

 _____

5. Most roads have white lines along each side. What do you think they are for?

 _____

 _____

1. A construction crew painted dashed lines along a stretch of road that is 320 feet long. If each dashed line is 10 feet long and there is 10 feet in between each line, how many dashed lines did the crew paint?

_____ lines

2. A construction crew painted 45 dashed lines along a stretch of road. If each dashed line is 3 meters long and there is 3 meters in between each line, how long was the stretch of road?

_____ meters

Clean up the trail of milk left behind the wagon. Follow the path through the numbers that are divisible by 3.

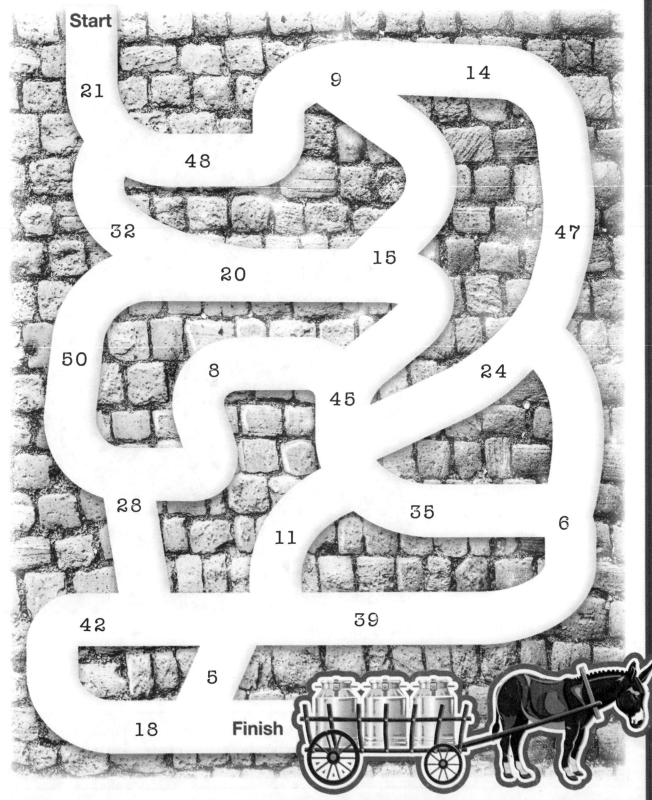

Be careful where you plant a tree! Trees want to grow. If something is in its way, a tree will just grow around or through or over it.

Such was the curious case of a bicycle in Scotland. It will never be ridden again. A tree has grown through it. The front wheel and handlebars look good. So does the back wheel. But the seat has rings of tree and bark around it. Some say the bike was chained there long ago when a young man went off to war.

Tourists visit another bike tree on an island in Washington. An old man says he left the bike there decades ago because it was too small for him. Today, the bicycle is stuck in a tree, seven feet (2 m) off the ground.

A RIDE GOING NOWHERE

Trees have grown around toys, cars, rocks, golf balls, cemetery stones, ice skates, park benches, road signs, and even a motorcycle. The most common thing trees "eat" is fences. Don't worry about the trees. They're just fine.

 **FUN FACT** There is a word for what happens when a tree grows around an obstacle. It is *edaphoecotropism*. Can you say it? Try it.

1. What is the main idea of this text?

_____

_____

2. Name three key details that support the main idea.

_____

_____

_____

_____

3. Write a different title for this passage.

_____

4. Name the three most surprising items trees have grown around.

_____

_____

_____

1. The arborist studied a slice of a tree. She cuts out a piece that is a 30° angle. If she cuts the same size pieces, how many pieces will she cut in all?

_____ pieces

2. The arborist studied a slice of a tree. She cuts the slice into six equal pieces. How many degrees is the angle of each piece?

_____ degrees

3. The arborist studies two tree slices. Tree Slice A is cut into ten equal pieces. Tree Slice B is cut into equal pieces whose angles are 20°. Which tree slice has more pieces? Explain.

Tree Slice A

Tree Slice B

_____

_____

_____

Circle the objects hidden in the tree.

| teddy bear | street sign | football | car | fence | baseball glove | bicycle |

You hear a horse gallop in a cowboy movie. But, the sound may not be horse hooves. It is probably a sound effect. Galloping noise is often made with coconut shells. Clip clop, clip clop!

OW!

Making sound effects is an art. Before TV, there were radio shows. Voices could tell the story. Add the sound of creaking doors or quiet breathing, and it's a scary story.

Sound artists need good imaginations. Take *Jurassic Park*. No one has ever heard a dinosaur breathe or roar. So, sound artists used real animal sounds. They twisted them on a computer. T. rex breathing? That was a whale. The T. rex roar came from tigers, lions, elephants, and alligators.

Snow sounds are often made by squishing corn starch. Gloves tipped with paper clips sound like dog paws. Breaking a stalk of celery sounds like a bone breaking. Shaking a pair of gloves imitates bird wings flapping. These and many more sound effects are recorded with a microphone and added to a movie. And you thought they were real!

 **FUN FACT**

The laser blasts in *Star Wars* were made by hitting tightly stretched wires with a hammer. Darth Vader breathed through scuba gear. Chewbacca's roar was modeled after a walrus cry.

Match each word to its definition.

1. gallop   to copy what something or someone does

2. effect   the ability to see something in one's mind

3. imagination   something that was caused to happen

4. imitate   to move or run quickly

Write a response to the question.

5. Why do you think people who create sounds are called *artists*?

_____

_____

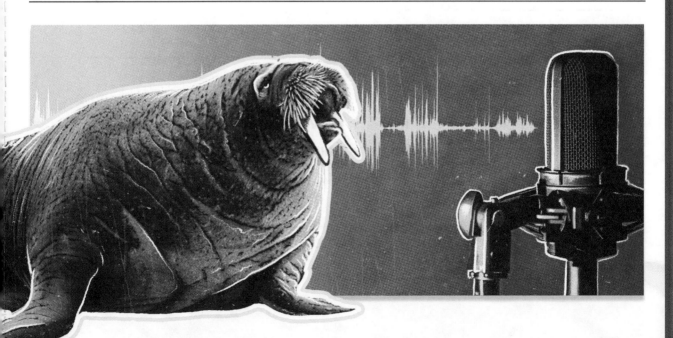

Solve each problem.

1. You are a sound artist and the director of the movie needs you to make different sounds. If it takes an average of 1.5 days to record 15 sounds, about how many sounds could you make in one work week?

_____ sounds

2. You finish recording the 30 sounds for the movie on May 21st. If you complete 1.5 sounds per day, on which date did you start recording?

_____

3. On Monday you record 23 sounds. On Tuesday you record 31 sounds. On Wednesday you record 18 sounds. How many sounds did you record in total? Explain two ways you could solve for the answer.

_____ sounds

_____

4. Over one year you made 6,750 sounds for 16 different movies. About how many sounds did you make for each movie? (Assume you made the same amount for each movie.) About how many sounds per day did you record?

_____ sounds for each movie

_____ sounds per day

Follow the directions.

You are hired to create the sounds for each action in a scene. Write the name of each object you would use to make the sound needed for each action. Then, include an estimated amount of time.

Action	Objects Used	Total Time in Scene
Restaurant door swings opens		
Door closes		
Woman in high heels walks quickly toward a table		
Woman sits down forcefully into padded vinyl booth bench		
Dishes are being washed in the background		
Woman opens the menu and flips the pages		

1. How much total time did you estimate for this scene?

_____

2. If the director asks you to cut the time in half, what might you do? Explain.

_____

FRUIT OR VEG?

Let's talk about fruit and vegetable lies. Take tomatoes, for example. Tomatoes are not vegetables. They are fruit. To be more exact, they are berries. They have lots of seeds and no stone. The same goes for eggplants, cucumbers, and bell peppers. And this will blow your mind. A banana is a berry, but a strawberry is not. That's because strawberry seeds are on the outside.

There are many fruit and vegetable lies. Not all oranges are orange. Some are green or yellow. Oranges do have plenty of Vitamin C, but kiwifruit has more. Apples are part of the rose family. So are apricots, cherries, and pears. Lettuce is a big, green, leafy surprise. It is related to sunflowers and daisies.

Finally, Popeye was wrong about spinach. It doesn't really make you stronger. Still, eat your spinach. It's good for you.

 **FUN FACT** The fear of vegetables is called *lachanophobia*. It's real. Some people have trouble breathing or want to vomit when they see broccoli or carrots.

Write T for _true_ or F for _false_.

_____ 1. Strawberries are a kind of berry.

_____ 2. Tomatoes are a juicy, red vegetable.

_____ 3. Kiwifruit have more vitamin C than oranges.

_____ 4. Apples are part of the rose family.

_____ 5. Spinach makes you stronger.

Write a response to the question.

6. Name at least one food you don't like or are afraid of. Explain.

_____

_____

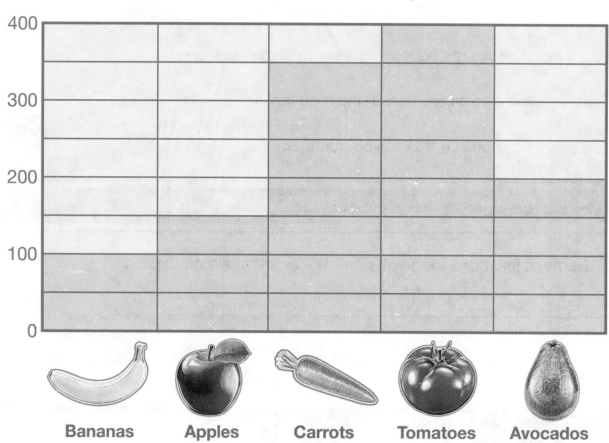

Mae's Market Stand Weekly Order

Mae's Market Stand Weekly Order	
Bananas	
Apples	
Carrots	
Tomatoes	
Avocados	

Find the names of 10 fruits and vegetables in the puzzle.

TOMATO		CUCUMBER
EGGPLANT		BANANA
PEPPER		STRAWBERRY
APPLE		SPINACH
LETTUCE		APRICOT

```
A  I  S  R  M  R  M  T  J  O  T  S  A  L
D  G  B  S  P  I  N  A  C  H  O  W  H  L
S  D  B  N  M  A  T  J  M  Z  M  W  Y  E
T  W  Q  E  L  F  H  S  I  Y  A  U  I  T
G  F  S  P  N  M  D  T  O  P  T  L  J  T
S  D  G  G  H  A  P  R  I  C  O  T  K  U
P  G  B  V  U  A  E  A  H  O  P  T  R  C
E  Y  I  O  H  B  K  W  X  C  V  B  N  E
P  D  G  H  M  J  K  B  A  N  A  N  A  O
P  I  O  U  B  V  C  E  G  N  M  U  P  I
E  E  C  V  B  N  M  R  O  P  T  R  P  C
R  U  G  E  W  E  F  R  H  J  K  M  L  V
C  X  C  V  B  H  G  Y  W  J  K  A  E  S
```

CTC, ANYONE?

CTC means "care to chat" on a cell phone. Texting language can be fun. If you have a cell phone, you probably know a lot of words. *LOL* means "laughing out loud." *IDK* stands for "I don't know." *BRB* means "be right back." And *JK* stands for "just kidding."

Another familiar text phrase is *OMG*, which stands for "Oh My God!" No one knows when it first became popular. But, it is surprising to learn it was first used way back in 1917! This was long before cell phones. The abbreviation was written in a letter to Winston Churchill, who would later become the prime minister of England.

FUN FACT

The first text message ever was sent in 1992. The message simply said, "Merry Christmas."

OMG!

Churchill was important in the British Royal Navy during World War I. This letter was written by a powerful man in the Navy, Lord John Arbuthnot Fisher. Lord Fisher had just retired from the Navy. He didn't like its war plans. He wrote "O.M.G." in an angry letter. Behind it, he wrote "(Oh! My God!) in case Churchill didn't know what O.M.G. meant.

Write two different meanings for each word from the passage.

1. text

_____

_____

2. letter

_____

_____

Answer each question.

3. What does the author mean by the phrase *texting language*?

   A. the language people speak in Texas

   B. the abbreviations used to text on cell phones

   C. the way sentences are formed in a passage

4. Why did Lord Fisher write "OMG" in a letter to Churchill?

   A. Lord Fisher thought Churchill was unwell.

   B. Lord Fisher wanted to congratulate Churchill on winning the war.

   C. Lord Fisher was quite upset with the Navy's war plans.

Solve each problem. (Note: The character limit of a text is 168.)

1. How many more characters could Jess use if her text is at 145 characters?

   _____ characters

2. Kyle has 38 characters left to use in his text. How many characters long is his text now?

   _____ characters

3. Lexi receives a text that is cut off. It is 42 characters too long. How many characters are in the text?

   _____ characters

4. Henry writes a text that is 84 characters long. He deletes half of the characters. Then, he adds to his text. His final text is 157 characters long. How many characters did he add to his text?

   _____ characters

5. Your mom texts you every hour of your six-hour-long field trip. About how long is each text if she texts a total of 858 characters?

   _____ characters

1	2	3	4	5	6	7	8	9	10	11	12	13
A	B	C	D	E	F	G	H	I	J	K	L	M

14	15	16	17	18	19	20	21	22	23	24	25	26
N	O	P	Q	R	S	T	U	V	W	X	Y	Z

DO ___ WANT TO TALK ___ ___? ___ ___ ___.
21 ... 18 14 ... 12 13 11

GETTING COFFEE ___ ___ ___ ___. ___ ___ ___.
1 19 1 16 ... 2 18 2

___ ___. ___ ___ ___, CAN YOU GET ME ONE?
14 16 ... 2 20 23

YES. ___ ___ ___.
9 15 21

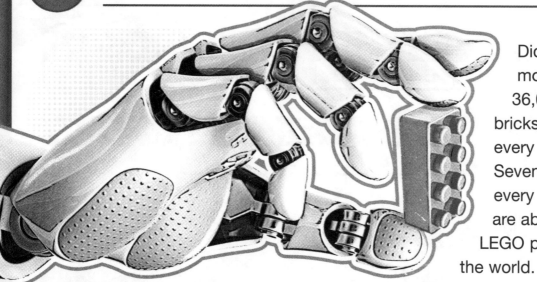

Did you know more than 36,000 LEGO® bricks are made every minute? Seven sets are sold every second. There are about 400 billion LEGO pieces around the world.

Kids and adults use LEGO blocks to build trains, robots, dogs, race cars, and dinosaurs. Some LEGO creations will make your eyes pop. The Guinness World Record for the largest LEGO statue goes to a 42-foot-long copy of London's Tower Bridge. It was made with 5,805,845 pieces!

FUN FACT

Brickley, the LEGO sea serpent, can be seen in Disney Springs, Florida. He is 30 feet (9 m) long and was made in 1997 with 170,000 LEGO bricks.

Another jaw-dropping LEGO wonder is the Kennedy Space Center. Using 750,000 bricks, it includes a 6.13-foot-tall space shuttle and launch pad plus a 6-foot-tall vehicle assembly building. It took 2,500 hours to build! And then there's the Saturn V rocket. Taking 250 hours and using 120,000 bricks, the rocket stood 12 feet tall. Look closely to see R2-D2 and C-3PO near the top.

A team of five built a full-sized car with 201,016 LEGO pieces in 2014. It weighed 2,930 pounds! A classic Volkswagen camper was built with over 400,000 LEGO pieces. It weighed 1,543 pounds. That's a lot of LEGO bricks at play!

Write F for *fact* or O for *opinion*.

_____ 1. More than 36,000 LEGO blocks are made every minute.

_____ 2. Some LEGO creations will make your eyes pop.

_____ 3. A camper was built with over 400,000 LEGO pieces.

_____ 4. That's a lot of LEGO bricks!

Write a response to each question.

5. What new information did you learn in this passage?

_____

_____

6. Write about an experience you or a friend has had with LEGO blocks.

_____

_____

LOTS AND LOTS AND LOTS OF LEGOS

1. A team is working on a new LEGO creation. They have 842 LEGO bricks. They need 167 times as many. How many total LEGO bricks do they need?

   _____ LEGO bricks

2. A team wants to build an even bigger LEGO sea serpent. They have 751 LEGO bricks. They need 468 times as many. How many LEGO bricks do they need in all?

   _____ LEGO bricks

3. A team has 432 LEGO bricks to make 24 creations. How many bricks do they have per creation if they split them evenly?

   _____ LEGO bricks

4. A team has 936 LEGO bricks to make 36 creations. How many bricks do they have per creation if they split them evenly?

WATCH YOUR STEP!

   _____ LEGO bricks

Fill in the missing numbers from bottom to top. The sum of two numbers should appear in the brick straddled above those two bricks.

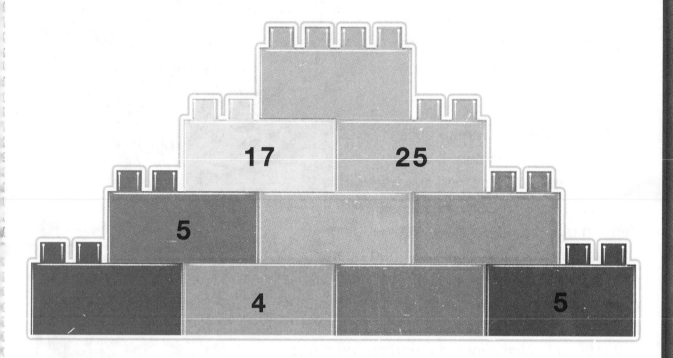

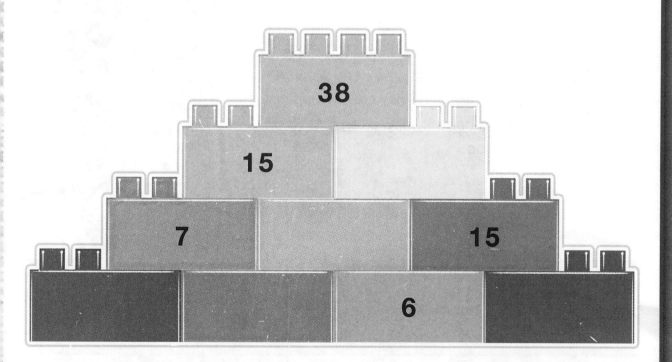

CARATS OR CARROTS?

What is the difference between a carat and a carrot? Diamonds and other gemstones are measured in carats. Carrots, that you eat, are a whole other thing. So, why are so many diamond rings showing up on carrots?

In 2011, a Swedish woman pulled up a carrot in her garden. It was "wearing" the diamond ring she had lost 16 years before. In 2016, an 82-year-old German man found his long-lost wedding ring wrapped around a carrot. It had been missing for three years. In 2017, a Canadian woman was pulling weeds in her garden. She discovered the ring she'd lost 13 years earlier. In 2018, an English woman found her gold ring in the carrot patch. It had been a birthday gift 12 years earlier.

What a mystery! But maybe not, since the rings were lost in their gardens. That's easy to do when you're working in the dirt with your hands. Next time you're pulling up carrots, pay attention! And, maybe wear gloves too.

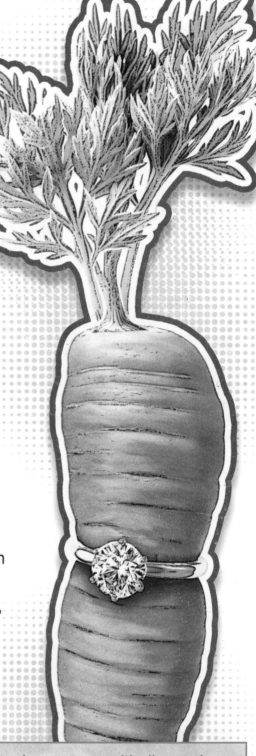

FUN FACT

Most carrots do not come with diamond rings wrapped around them! But they do come in a variety of colors such as purple, red, white, yellow, and orange.

Write a response to each question.

1. What is the difference between a *carat* and a *carrot*?

_____

_____

2. Summarize the text in two or three sentences.

_____

_____

3. How are the people in this text alike? How are they different?

_____

_____

_____

Match each ring description to the country it was found in.

4. 82-year-old man's wedding ring   England

5. ring lost 13 years earlier   Sweden

6. diamond ring lost 16 years earlier   Canada

7. gold ring given as birthday gift   Germany

Write the fraction and decimal for the shaded part of each figure.

A garden is filled with lost rings! With each carrot harvest, a fraction of the carrots come up with rings. The shaded parts of each figure show the fraction of carrots with rings.

1.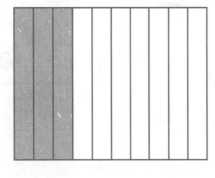

_____ _____

2.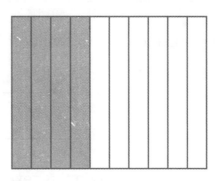

_____ _____

3.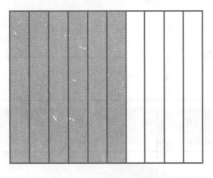

_____ _____

4.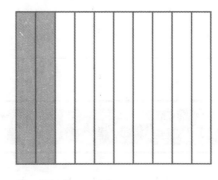

_____ _____

5.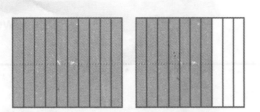

_____ _____

6.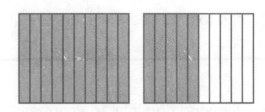

_____ _____

Follow the directions.

Draw rings on the carrots whose numbers are multiples of 7.

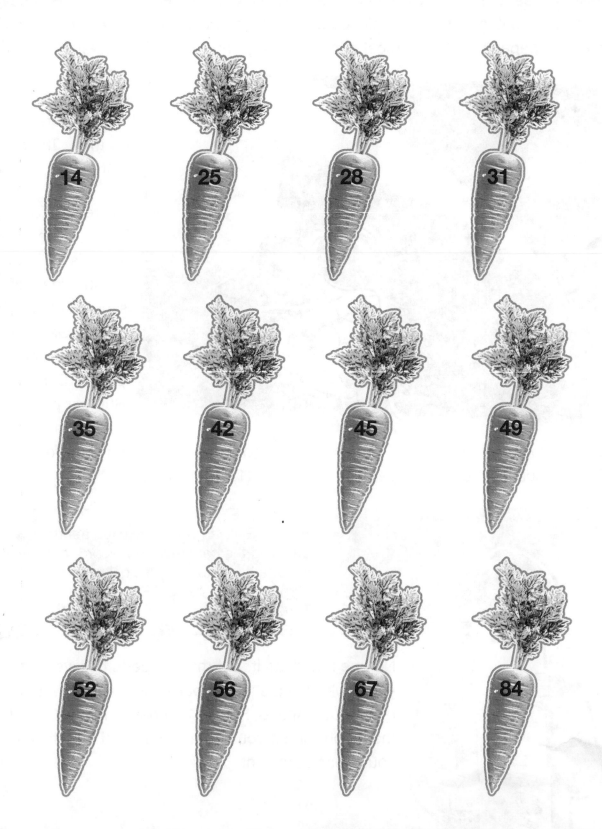

14 25 28 31

35 42 45 49

52 56 67 84

Take a sheet of paper. Fold it in half. Fold it in half again. How many more times can you fold it in half? You think you could go on forever. It's very easy to fold a piece of paper in half. But, most people will say you can't fold a sheet of paper more than seven, maybe eight, times. It gets too thick. Try it yourself!

The record for folding a piece of paper is 12 times. An American high school student, Britney Gallivan, folded a piece of paper 12 times. But, her piece of paper was toilet paper. Does that count? Yes! But she needed to find a very long hall for folding. That's because the toilet paper was 4,000 feet (1,219 m) long.

FUN FACT

Britney Gallivan was so excited about breaking the paper-folding record that she wrote a book about it. It's called, no surprise, "How to Fold Paper in Half 12 Times."

No one has done it, but math experts believe that if you could fold a sheet of paper 30 times, it would reach outer space. Fold it 42 times, and it will touch the moon. And if you find a way to fold it 50 times, it could reach the sun.

1. What did you find most surprising in this passage?

_____

_____

2. The author says you can only fold a sheet of paper seven or eight times. Yet, a student folded a piece of toilet paper 12 times. How could both be true?

_____

_____

_____

Complete each sentence with a number from the number bank.

12	30	42	50

3. The record for folding a piece of paper is _____ times.

4. If you could fold it _____ times, you might reach the sun.

5. If you could fold it _____ times, it might touch the moon.

6. If you could fold it _____ times, you might reach outer space.

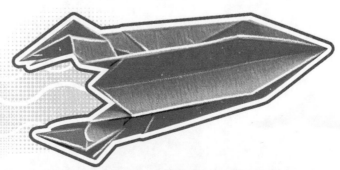

Draw lines to show the folds in each problem. Write the fraction names.

1. Fold the paper in half 2 times.
What is the paper divided into?

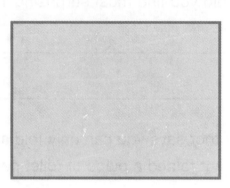

_____

2. Fold the paper in half 3 times.
What is the paper divided into?

_____

3. Fold the paper in half 4 times.
What is the paper divided into?

_____

Follow the directions to make a paper airplane.

1. Get a piece of paper.

2. Fold the paper in half.

3. Unfold and then fold in the top two corners to the center fold line.

4. Fold down the top point to the center line to create a square.

5. Fold the top two corners to the center about an inch above the downward facing point.

6. Fold the downward facing point up.

7. Fold the plane in half.

8. Fold the edges down to create the wings.

FINISHED PAPER AIRPLANE

The most common letter in the English language is *e*. Try writing a whole sentence without using this letter. It's almost impossible!

Still, a book named *Gadsby* was written in 1939 without the letter *e*. Only the introduction and the author's name, Ernest Vincent Wright, contained this common letter. But, they were not part of the story and don't count.

FUN FACT

A written work, such as a book or an essay, that leaves out certain letters on purpose is called a *lipogram*.

The book was 260 pages long. Imagine how difficult it must have been to write such a long book without using that reoccurring letter. Think of the words Wright had to leave out, such as *the*, *he*, *she*, *they*, and *we*. We use these common words all the time in our writing. Just count how many words in this short passage contain an *e*. Yet, Wright wrote an entire book without the letter we all use so much. We could call him a hero if it didn't have an *e* in it!

Write a response for each question.

1. Write three facts from the text about the book *Gadsby*.

_____

_____

_____

2. Including the title, how many words in this passage contain the letter *e*?

_____

3. Write a sentence about yourself without using the letter *e*.

_____

_____

Write an antonym for each word.

4. whole _____

5. introduction _____

6. common _____

WHAT STARTS
WITH E, ENDS WITH E,
AND HAS ONLY ONE
LETTER IN IT?

AN ENVELOPE!

Solve each problem.

1. The first book in a trilogy has 1,736 ☺'s. The second book has 2,946 ☺'s. The last book has 4,507 ☺'s. How many total ☺'s are in the trilogy?

_____ ☺'s

2. A story about a dragon has 5,632 ☺'s. A story about a pilot has 3,821 ☺'s. How many more ☺'s does the dragon story have than the pilot story?

_____ ☺'s

3. The book Sophia is reading has 6,004 ☺'s. Her little sister is reading a book with 27 ☺'s. Her brother is reading a book with 591 ☺'s. How many total ☺'s are in the siblings' books?

A, B, C, D, F, G...

_____ ☺'s

4. Oliver wrote an essay and used 806 ☺'s. Liam wrote an essay and used 550 ☺'s. How many more ☺'s did Oliver use than Liam?

_____ ☺'s

There are special sentences that use every letter in the alphabet. These are called *pangrams*. One popular pangram is below.

1	2	3	4	5	6	7	8	9	10	11	12	13
A	B	C	D	E	F	G	H	I	J	K	L	M

14	15	16	17	18	19	20	21	22	23	24	25	26
N	O	P	Q	R	S	T	U	V	W	X	Y	Z

___ ___ ___
20   8   5

___ ___ ___ ___ ___   ___ ___ ___ ___ ___
17 21 9 3 11   2 18 15 23 14

___ ___ ___   ___ ___ ___ ___ ___
6 15 24   10 21 13 16 19

___ ___ ___ ___   ___ ___ ___
15 22 5 18   20 8 5

___ ___ ___ ___   ___ ___ ___.
12 1 26 25   4 15 7

NUKE WHAT!?

Do you ever wonder how things are invented? Does someone just think, "Ice cream should be cold. I'll invent a freezer"? Sometimes it works like that. Inventors see a problem and then invent a solution.

But, the microwave oven was invented by accident in 1946. A scientist, Percy Spencer, was testing a special tube for the military. Then, he took a break. He liked to feed squirrels on his break and always had a chocolate peanut bar in his pocket. When he pulled it out on this day, it had melted!

FUN FACT

The first microwave was called the Radarange. It cost nearly $5,000 and weighed a whopping 750 pounds (340 kg).

Percy guessed this gooey mess might have to do with the tubes he was working on. So, he stuck an egg under the tube. A few minutes later, it splattered all over his face! The next day he brought in popping corn and was able to share popcorn with the whole office. The microwave oven was born, all because of some melted squirrel treats.

Write a response to each question.

1. Who is Percy Spencer and why is he important?

_____

_____

_____

2. How did a squirrel become part of the invention of a microwave?

_____

_____

_____

_____

Write two different meanings for each word from the passage.

3. wonder

_____

_____

4. break

_____

_____

1. If 5 neighbors each bought one of the first microwave ovens at a price of $5,000 each, how much money did the neighbors spend in all?

$ _____

2. How many of the first microwave ovens could a cafeteria buy if they had $15,000 to spend?

_____ microwave ovens

3. Percy popped 9 bags of popcorn. Each bag had 100 kernels. How many kernels were popped in all?

_____ kernels

4. Percy popped 250 kernels. Each bag of popcorn had 50 kernels. How many bags of popcorn could he hand out?

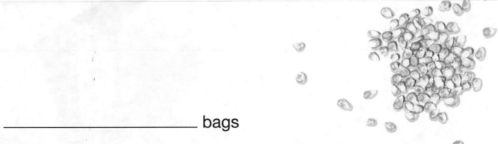

_____ bags

Solve the maze. Write the letters you cross in order on the lines below to reveal a fun fact!

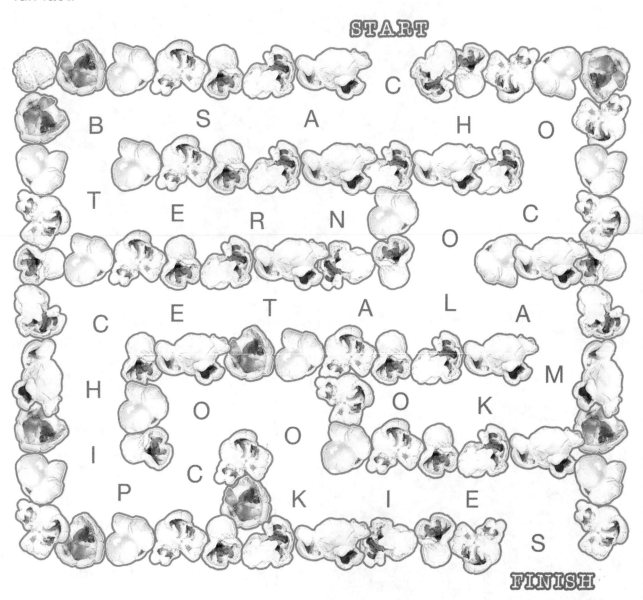

Microwaves weren't the only thing invented by accident! The first

_____ _____ _____ _____ _____ _____ _____

_____ _____ _____ _____

_____ _____ _____ _____ _____ _____

were a delicious accident.

Pancakes look like circles. Pizza slices come in triangles. Now, name a food that is square. Huh? Believe it or not, more foods are square than you think. Some crackers, waffles, and cheese are square. They come from the factory that way. What about square fruits or vegetables? Or square eggs?

FUN FACT

A new company called SquarEat will deliver square food to your door. Square chicken patties, square hamburgers, and all kinds of square vegetables are on the menu.

Animals do not lay square eggs. But you could make a boiled egg square if you put it in a box when it was still warm. You could actually grow square tomatoes, pumpkins, and squash if you boxed them as they started growing. This would be a lot of work and stores would have to charge more for their produce. And what if the square veggies tasted bad?

Square watermelons are popular in Japan. They are grown in boxes. As the watermelon grows it takes the shape of the box it is in. Their cubical shapes make them easier to transport, store, and slice. Yum!

1. What was the author's purpose in writing this passage?

   A. to inform

   B. to entertain

   C. to persuade

2. Why did the author say, "more foods are square than you think"?

   A. Many popular foods, such as apples and eggs, are round.

   B. Stores don't carry square foods.

   C. Square foods are only made in factories.

Write a response to each question.

3. Why do you think that cubical watermelons are easier to transport and store?

   _____

   _____

   _____

4. What food would you **not** buy if it came as a cube? Explain.

   _____

   _____

   _____

Find the volume of each watermelon.

Volume is found by multiplying the length, width, and height of a figure.

1.

3 ft.
2 ft.
2 ft.

_____

2.

8 in.
6 in.
7 in.

_____

3.

2 ft.
4 ft.
5 ft.

_____

4.

9 in.
12 in.
10 in.

_____

Find your way through the maze to the center of the watermelon. Watch out for the seeds!

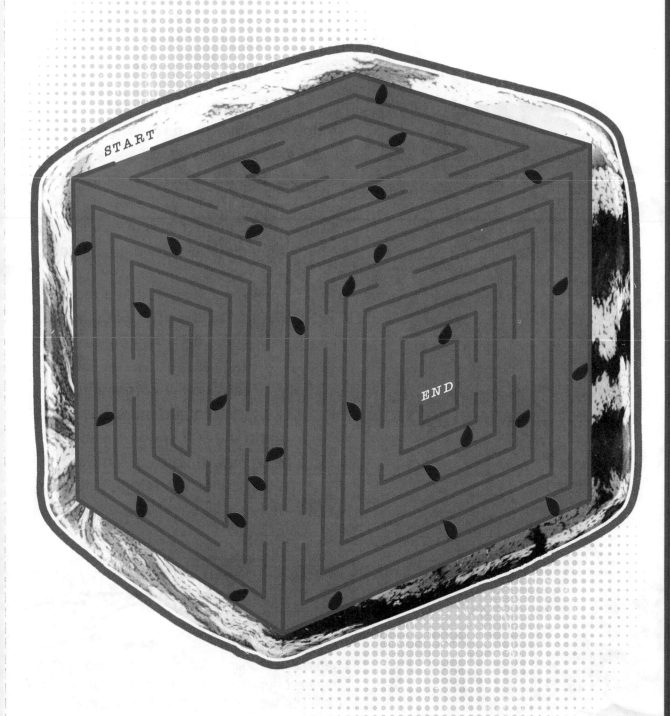

TROLL BRIDGE

You probably remember the hungry troll in *The Three Billy Goats Gruff*. He lived under a bridge and popped out whenever someone crossed it. Then, he promised to eat them. But, trolls only exist in Norse fairy tales.

In Portland, Oregon, you can visit a troll bridge. Hanging on an old wooden railroad bridge, you will see a mix of tiny troll dolls. Some people have painted trolls on the wood. But, most are real troll dolls with wild, tangled hair and happy faces.

A local story is that a mom started the troll bridge by putting troll dolls on the bridge to surprise her kids. People in the community started to add more troll dolls and the troll bridge was born! Portland, Oregon, is famous for its art scene. The bridge just adds to the fun.

FUN FACT

The first troll dolls were made of wood. They had bushy hair made from sheep's wool. The wool was dyed either black, white, or orange.

Write a response to each question.

1. How did the troll bridge start?

_____

_____

2. What connections can you make between this text and another you have read?

_____

_____

3. Would you want to visit a troll bridge? Explain.

_____

_____

Answer the question.

4. Which is **not** a meaning of the word *wild* in this passage?

A. beautiful

B. messy

C. untamed

BAD HAIR DAY

Write the best unit of measure for each troll's travels.

These trolls are on the move!

1 foot = 12 inches

1 yard = 3 feet

1 mile = 1,760 yards or 5,280 feet

1. This troll is going from Portland, Oregon, to Gatlinburg, Tennessee.

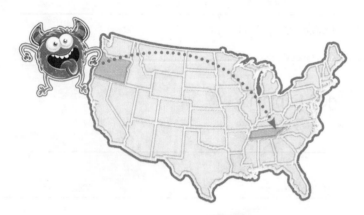

_____

2. This troll is going from one side of the bridge to the other.

_____

3. This troll is running down a football field. Touchdown!

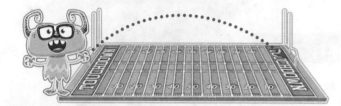

_____

Use the code to reveal the fun fact.

1	2	3	4	5	6	7	8	9	10	11	12	13
A	B	C	D	E	F	G	H	I	J	K	L	M

14	15	16	17	18	19	20	21	22	23	24	25	26
N	O	P	Q	R	S	T	U	V	W	X	Y	Z

Take a hike in Breckenridge, Colorado, if you'd like to come face-to-face with a

15-foot-tall __ __ __ __ __ __   __ __ __ __ __ !
          23 15 15 4 5 14   20 18 15 12 12

The hiking trail is called the

__ __ __ __ __ __ __ __ __ __ __
20 18 15 12 12 19 20 9 7 5 14

__ __ __ __ __   and the   __ __ __ __ __ __ __
20 18 1 9 12   20 18 15 12 12 19

__ __ __ __   __ __
14 1 13 5   9 19

__ __ __ __
9 19 1 11

__ __ __ __ __ __ __ __ __ __ .
8 5 1 18 20 19 20 15 14 5

LET ME DRIVE!

Let's dig a hole with a big, yellow digger. Would you rather ride in a real dump truck? Or scoop up dirt with a mini digger? You can climb, drive, and ride in big equipment at Diggerland USA. It was the first construction-themed amusement park built in the United States. It's in New Jersey.

Diggerland has 25 rides and includes a petting zoo, water park, zipline, rock wall, and more. But the best part is the big machines. You can climb on a tractor or skid-steer loader and drive it around a track yourself. Have fun picking up and moving shapes around with a crazy crane. The Spin Dizzy whirls passengers up and down and around in a huge digger bucket. Tighten your seatbelt! Then, take turns driving behind the wheel of a backhoe.

Diggerland was the first park of its kind in the United States. But, it is not the last. More construction-themed parks are popping up. Dig World is a new park built in Texas in 2022. And guess what?
A lot of it was built with real diggers!

FUN FACT

Tickets to Diggerland USA are pricey. But if you have straight A's on your report card, you'll get a discount!

Complete each sentence with a word from the word bank.

| construction | equipment | machines | seatbelt |

1. The theme at this park is _____.

2. You can climb, drive, and ride in big _____ at
   Diggerland.

3. Be sure to wear your _____ on the _____.

Write two different meanings for each word from the passage.

4. park

   _____

   _____

5. scoop

   _____

   _____

Solve each problem.

1. Sam is buying two tickets to Diggerland USA. She gets one on sale for $45.95 but the other she pays full price for at $49.95. How much does Sam spend on tickets?

$ _____

2. Wyatt gets a season pass to Diggerland USA for $129.95. Ethan gets a single day pass for $45.95. How much more does Wyatt spend than Ethan?

$ _____

3. A family of 4 goes to Diggerland USA. One of the kids is under 36 inches tall and does not need a ticket. The rest of the family's tickets cost $45.95 each. How much does the family spend?

$ _____

4. Jolie goes to Diggerland USA in August and spends $49.95 on her ticket. Hana goes in September and spends $46.95 on her ticket. How much more does Jolie spend than Hana?

$ _____

UNUSU

Find 8 names of some popular construction equipment in the puzzle.

EXCAVATOR

BULLDOZER

GRADER

PAVER

COMPACTOR

BACKHOE

TRENCHER

LOADER

A Q W D F V G B H P A V E R I
S R B C D F V B N H G J X M L
C V B B N G L K O P H G C N M
Q C A U F D S A R G D G A G H
W X C Z L C V B R N M L V L K
T I K U Y L Q A S D L F A G H
R J H K L K D F E R O B T K J
E Z O V S E D O I O A P O L K
N X E C R V B N Z M D P R O I
C U I G H J K K L E E R T Y U
H Q C O M P A C T O R I U T R
E M N I V D F B W E R T G V C
R M N V M E H J O E W Q U I O

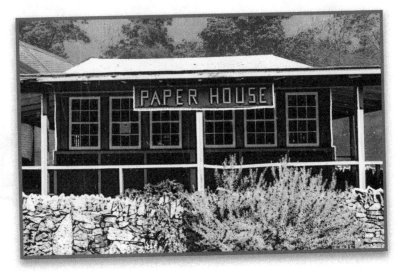

What's black and white and "read" all over? A newspaper, right? But no, it's the Rockport Paper House in Massachusetts. This unusual home has the usual wood frame and roof. But the walls, doors, and even the furniture are made from newspapers. About 100,000 of them!

The paper house was built by Elis Stenman in 1922. Its walls are about an inch thick. He stuck 215 layers together with a paste made of water, flour, and apple peels. He painted the walls with varnish. It made the newspapers stiff and kept them from tearing. Even the furniture is made from rolled newspapers. The table, chairs, desk, and sofa were all created from newsprint. So were the lamps, the curtains, a bookshelf, and a grandfather clock.

The Stenmans lived in the paper house for five years during the summer months. It had running water, electricity, and a stove. Like many other homes from that era, there was no indoor bathroom. Instead, they used an outhouse. It was not made of paper. But hopefully, it contained some paper!

FUN FACT The paper house includes a working fireplace, but no one has ever lit a fire in it. Who wants to build a fire near that much paper?

Answer each question.

1. How was each wall of the paper house made?

   A. with wooden beams

   B. with 215 layers of newspaper

   C. with sheets of plywood

2. What did Stenman use to keep the newspaper layers together?

   A. wallpaper paste

   B. school glue

   C. a paste made of water, flour, and apple peels

Write a response to each question.

3. What did the author mean by saying of the outhouse, "hopefully, it contained some paper"?

   _____

   _____

4. What feature of the paper house would you most like to see? Explain.

   _____

   _____

Find the perimeter and area of each room.

Perimeter is the distance around a figure. It is found by adding all the sides. **Area** is the total space taken up by an object. It is found by multiplying the length times the width.

1.

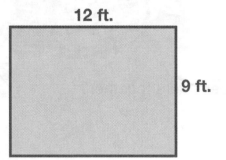

12 ft.

9 ft.

Perimeter _____

Area _____

2.

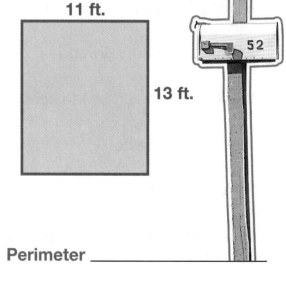

11 ft.

13 ft.

Perimeter _____

Area _____

3.

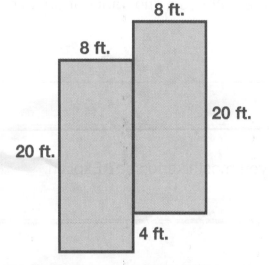

8 ft.

8 ft.

20 ft.

20 ft.

4 ft.

Perimeter _____

Area _____

4.

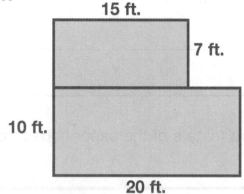

15 ft.

7 ft.

10 ft.

20 ft.

Perimeter _____

Area _____

Follow the directions.

The Paper House isn't the only home built with recycled materials! Solve the maze. Write the letters you cross in order on the lines below to discover what material makes up three houses on Prince Edward Island in Canada.

_____ _____ _____ _____ _____ _____

_____ _____ _____ _____ _____ _____ _____ _____

IT'S A HUGE MYSTERY!

One of the world's oldest mysteries is a place in England called *Stonehenge*. About 5,000 years ago, a circle was made of huge rock slabs. No one knows why. It took at least 1,000 years. How was it built without modern machines? The stones are huge. The lightest stones weigh nearly 8,000 pounds (3,600 kg). That's about the weight of a flatbed truck!

It would be fun to visit, but you don't have to go that far. An exact copy of Stonehenge was built out of foam. A sculptor walked into a factory that made huge foam blocks. He had an idea! He built Foamhenge in 10 days. You can see the attraction in Virginia.

If you live on the West Coast, check out Bunnyhenge in California. Fourteen large white bunnies sit in a circle, facing in. Two eight-foot bunnies stand off to the side, staring at each other. The bunnies cost the city $221,000. Visitors either like the stone bunnies or find them creepy. What do you think?

 **FUN FACT**   Another wacky Stonehenge replica is *Carhenge*. It is located in Nebraska and is built from vintage American automobiles covered in gray spray paint.

Match each attraction with its location.

1. Stonehenge   Nebraska

2. Foamhenge   California

3. Bunnyhenge   England

4. Carhenge   Virginia

Write a response to the question.

5. Which of the "henges" would you most like to see? Explain.

_____

_____

_____

One of the biggest mysteries around Stonehenge is how far the people of that time were able to travel with stones that heavy.

1 mile = 1.6 kilometers	**1 ton = 2,000 pounds**

1. The sandstone blocks forming the outer ring of Stonehenge came from 20 to 30 miles away. What is that distance range in kilometers?

   _____ kilometers

2. The volcanic bluestones in the inner ring in Stonehenge came from 256 kilometers away. What is the distance in miles?

   _____ miles

3. The average weight of a sandstone block is 25 tons. What is that weight in pounds?

   _____ pounds

4. The bluestones weigh between 4,000 and 10,000 pounds. What is that weight range in tons?

   _____ tons

Follow the directions.

There are many theories about how the stones got to Stonehenge. Choose a theory below you think is most likely and defend your choice.

1. Builders used wicker basketlike devices to transport the stones.

2. Builders created a way to slide the stones using balls and planks.

3. Glaciers moved the stones.

_____

_____

_____

_____

_____

_____

_____

_____

_____

_____

_____

_____

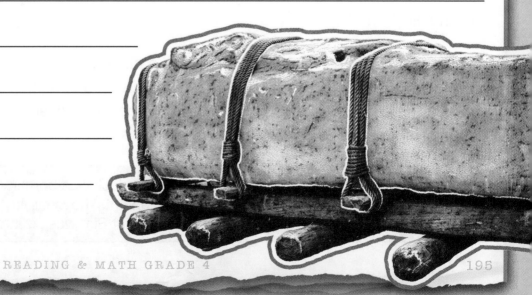

MR. TOILET HOUSE

Just when you think nothing else will surprise you, you see a house that looks like a toilet. Seriously!?

Welcome to Mr. Toilet House in Suwon, South Korea. Sim Jae-duck completed this toilet-shaped home in 2007. Sim was all about toilets. He wanted to improve toilet conditions around the world. He started by improving his town's restrooms. The town nicknamed him "Mr. Toilet."

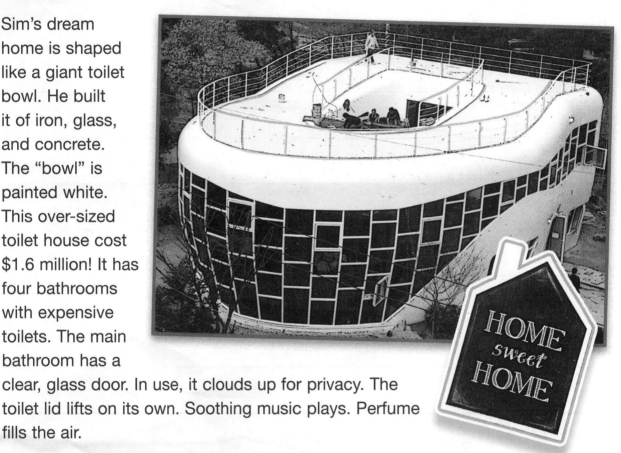

Sim's dream home is shaped like a giant toilet bowl. He built it of iron, glass, and concrete. The "bowl" is painted white. This over-sized toilet house cost $1.6 million! It has four bathrooms with expensive toilets. The main bathroom has a clear, glass door. In use, it clouds up for privacy. The toilet lid lifts on its own. Soothing music plays. Perfume fills the air.

HOME *sweet* HOME

Sim named his home *Haewoojae*, meaning a place to solve one's problems. A sign in front of the house reads, "Mr. Toilet House." Sim died in 2009. His family opened the home to visitors. Crowds tour the house. It even has a gift shop that sells toilet- and poop-themed gifts!

 **FUN FACT** Sim Jae-duck was born in a toilet of his grandparents' house. (Maybe this was the reason that Sim was so attached to toilets!?)

Write T for *true* or F for *false*.

_____ 1. The Mr. Toilet House is in North Korea.

_____ 2. Sim Jae-duck was born in a toilet.

_____ 3. The Mr. Toilet House cost $2.6 million.

_____ 4. *Haewoojae* means a place to wash your hands.

_____ 5. The gift shop sells toilet- and poop-themed gifts.

Write a response to the question.

6. Why do you think Sim Jae-duck built his home to look like a toilet? Explain.

_____

_____

_____

Answer each question.

1. Write 1.6 million in standard form.

   _____

2. The Mr. Toilet House gift shop sells $290,431 of toilet- and poop-shaped items each year. Write the number in expanded form.

   _____

3. Each year, the museum has a golden poop painting contest. In 2008, 256 children entered. In 2012, twice as many children entered the contest. And in 2016, five times as many children entered. How many more children entered in 2016 than in 2012?

   _____ more children

Use the information to write and solve your own problem.

   • The house takes up 1,994 square meters of land.

   • The first floor is 220.47 square meters.

   • The second floor is 138.73 square meters.

   _____

   _____

Follow the directions.

Cross out every other letter in each toilet name. Write the remaining letters on the lines. Then, write the circled letters in order to answer the question. The first one has been done for you.

1. P~~A~~R~~D~~I~~G~~V~~H~~Y~~S~~ P R I V (Y)

2. J M O U H C N ___ (_) ___ ___

3. L O A N T U R A I T N X E (_) ___ ___ ___ ___ ___ ___

4. L K O W O V ___ (_) ___

5. C T O J M Z M P O U D F E H ___ (_) ___ ___ ___ ___ ___

6. P S O L T B T D Y W ___ ___ (_)(_) ___

Question: What did one toilet say to the other?

Answer: __Y__ ___ U ___ ___ ___ K

A LI ___ ___ L E FLUSHED!

STICK YOUR GUM HERE!

You know you shouldn't throw chewing gum on the ground. That's called littering. People get their shoes stuck in it. Birds eat it and can die. Gum lasts forever. In

Singapore, you can go to jail for chewing gum for those reasons.

But, it's not against the law in Seattle, Washington. Just visit The Gum Wall. This sticky wall is covered with thousands of wads of chewing gum. The gum comes in all flavors and colors. The 50-foot-long wall is part of a theater building. People began sticking gum on the wall in the 1990s while waiting to get into the theater. At first, the theater cleaned it off. But every day, people stuck more gum there. It was too much work, so the theater just left it there.

FUN FACT

The Gum Wall was totally stripped of gum one time by the city. It took 130 hours. They scraped off 2,350 pounds (1,066 kg) of old and new gum. That's a ton of gum!

Today, it is a tourist attraction. People like to get their pictures taken in front of The Gum Wall. Some people think the colorful wall is gross. Other people like looking at the wall. And, most visitors with a stick of gum leave something behind. Would you?

Write a response to each question.

1. Describe The Gum Wall in Seattle, Washington.

_____

_____

_____

2. Write two reasons why gum is against the law in Singapore.

_____

_____

3. Do you think The Gum Wall is fun or gross? Explain.

_____

_____

Use each word in a sentence. Use the part of speech indicated.

4. wad (n) _____

_____

5. attraction (n) _____

_____

_____

Solve each problem.

1. It took workers 130 hours to remove 2,350 pounds of gum. About how many pounds of gum were removed each hour?

_____ pounds

2. If 5,000 new wads of gum are added to the wall each year from 1990 to the current year, how many wads of gum are there now?

_____ wads

3. In 2015, it was estimated that the wall held 1 million pieces of gum. About how many pieces of gum were added each year since 1990?

_____ pieces

4. If the wall of gum is 50 feet long, 70 feet wide, and 1 foot thick, then what is the volume of gum on the wall?

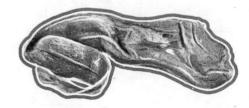

_____ cubic feet of gum

Follow the directions.

Let's play Gum-doku! Color the gum wads. Each row, column, and 2 x 3 rectangle of the gum wall must contain each color: red, orange, yellow, green, blue, and purple. The first rectangle has been done for you.

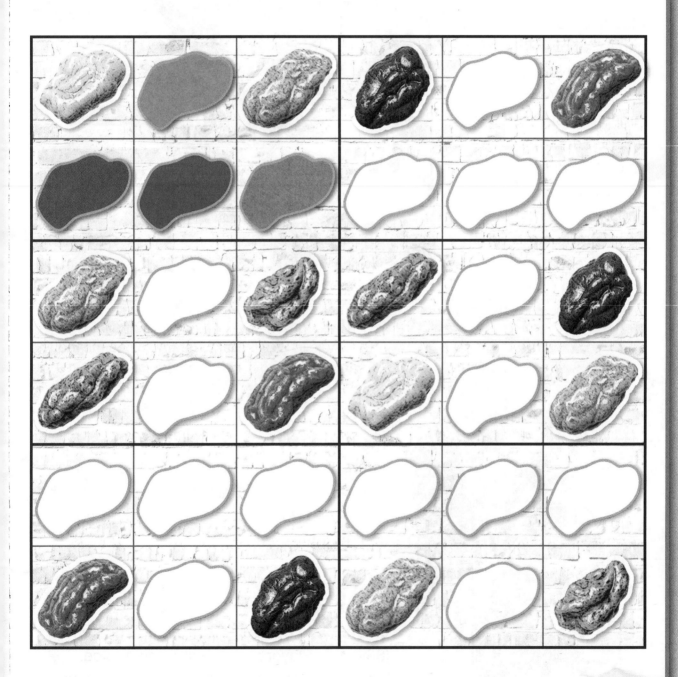

BOARD GAME GIANTS

Would you rather play checkers at a table or in a park on an oversized checkerboard? Let's go to Buffalo, New York. If you play, you can move giant checkers with your feet.

Kids and adults play large games all over the world. A town in Norway holds the record for the world's largest chess set. It's in a field. Each side is 87 yards (80 m) long. The squares are green (grass) and brown (dirt). Local people pretend to be chess pieces!

FUN FACT

The largest game of Jenga was built in Illinois in 2019. Giant Cat machines moved the 27 blocks. Each piece weighed about 600 pounds (272 kg).

The PAC-MAN Park in Seattle, Washington, is fun. The city painted part of a road there to look like the popular arcade game. You can be PAC-MAN. Run through the maze and gobble up the dots. Try not to be eaten by ghosts!

Next stop is the Monopoly in the Park game in San Jose, California. This granite Monopoly game board measures about 930 square feet (86.4 m²). Players roll a pair of giant dice. Wearing token-shaped hats, they walk their turns around the game board buying real estate, passing *Go*, and avoiding jail.

Match each giant game to its location.

1. checkers   Illinois

2. chess   California

3. PAC-MAN   Washington

4. Monopoly   New York

5. Jenga   Norway

Write a response to the question.

6. What game would you like to play in a giant size? Explain.

_____

_____

Solve each problem.

1. The largest chess board has sides that are 80 meters long each. Draw the shape of the game and label its perimeter and area.

2. The largest game of Monopoly takes up 930 square feet. If 30 square feet of the game space are damaged, how much is left? What could the perimeter be? Draw the new area and label the lengths of its sides and its perimeter.

3. What is the total weight of the largest game of Jenga? Use the information in the text to help you.

_____ pounds

Follow the directions.

Help your local park design a huge game board. The park has only 225 square feet of space to use. Draw the game and label the measurements.

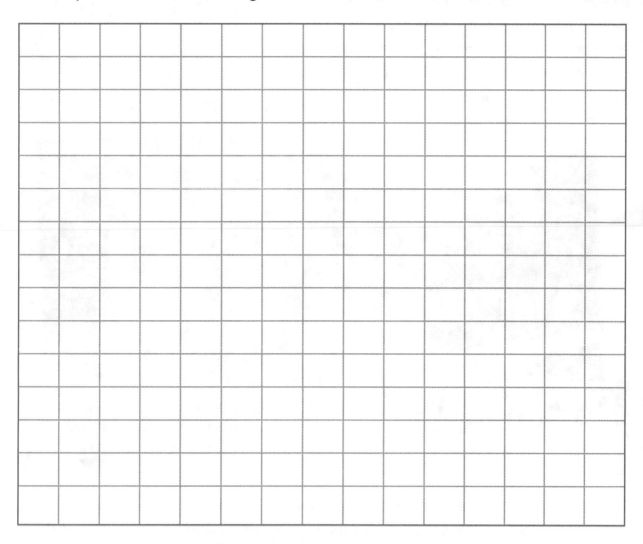

1 square unit = 1 square foot

BUNNY ISLAND

Yes, you really can visit a place where rabbits of all sizes and colors are the main event. In fact, they're the only event. Herds of wild rabbits hop all over the small island of Ōkunoshima off the coast of Japan. Most people today call it *Usagi Jima*, or Rabbit Island.

FUN FACT

A lot of people see a man in the moon when they look up. In Japan, they see a kindly rabbit making rice cakes with a hammer.

No one knows for sure how the bunnies came to be there. But, experts think some school kids released eight rabbits there in 1971. And, you know what they say about rabbits. They multiply! One rabbit can have 40 babies in one year.

Today, about 1,000 black, white, tan, and gray rabbits hop freely around the small island. When visitors step off the ferry, rabbits follow them around. Why? They're hungry. Rabbits can eat island grasses. But, there are lots of rabbits. They cannot eat people food. So, visitors feed them cabbage or other greens they get from the hotel there.

You can visit the rabbits for free. Don't be surprised if two or three dozen fluffy bunnies chase you through the park. On Usagi Jima, bunnies rule!

Write F for *fact* or O for *opinion*.

_____ 1. *Rabbit Island* is one nickname for the island of Ōkunoshima.

_____ 2. Experts think school kids released eight rabbits there.

_____ 3. There are a lot of rabbits.

_____ 4. Visitors feed the rabbits cabbage or other greens.

Write a response to the question.

5. Would you like to visit this island? Explain.

_____

_____

SOMEBUNNY LOVES VISITORS!

Solve each problem.

1. If one female rabbit can have about 40 bunnies each year, about how many bunnies would 500 rabbits have in one year?

_____ bunnies

2. You arrive at Rabbit Island and decide to walk around the island. The island is 4.3 kilometers in circumference. If it takes you 50 minutes to walk around the island, about how fast did you go? (Hint: speed = distance/time)

_____ km/h

Use the line graph to answer each question.

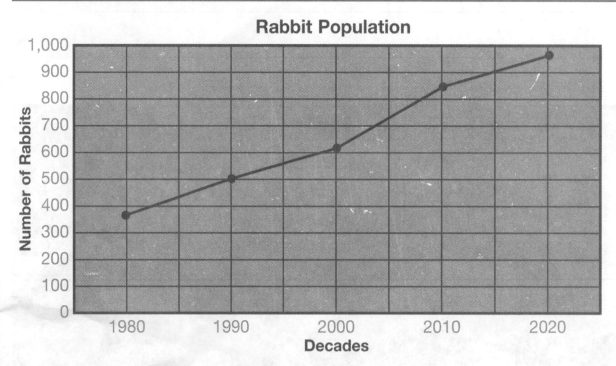

3. In what decade did the rabbit population grow the most? _____

4. In what decade did the rabbit population grow the least? _____

5. Which total is reasonable for 2030 if the population continues to grow?

995   1,190   2,800

Write the value of each bunny.

+ + = 36

× + = 36

÷ + = 4

+ × = _____

= _____   = _____   = _____

SAILING STONES

It makes sense that rocks may roll down a hill. But, what makes huge rocks roll on their own across a flat desert? Death Valley National Park is home to this great mystery. The park spreads across California and Nevada.

The rolling rocks are also called "sailing stones." Some have rolled as much as 1,500 feet (457 m). That's a long way for rocks to move on their own. Some are tiny. But, many weigh hundreds of pounds. No one has ever seen them roll. However, they leave trails in the sand. Rocks with smooth bottoms go this way and that. Those with rough bottoms roll in straight lines.

HEY, YOU! WANNA SEE HOW I ROLL?

FUN FACT

Some sailing stones have names. Karen weighs 700 pounds (318 kg). Hortense is fast and moved 820 feet (250 m) one winter. Other rocks are named Nancy, Alanis, Layla, Goldy, and Mary Ann.

At first, scientists thought the answer was a little gravity. Then, they saw many rocks were moving uphill. One scientist has studied the rolling rocks for years. She believes Death Valley weather may be the answer. In summer, it gets as hot as 120°F (49°C). In winter, it's cold and windy. She thinks the strong winds may be pushing the rocks across icy ground. That's one guess. What do you think?

Answer each question.

1. Where can you see sailing stones?

   A. on the Atlantic Ocean

   B. in the Galapagos Islands

   C. in Death Valley National Park

2. Death Valley spreads across which two states?

   A. California and Oregon

   B. Nevada and California

   C. Nevada and Arizona

3. How many people have seen the rocks roll?

   A. 25

   B. 6

   C. 0

4. How do scientists think the rocks have moved?

   A. They slid on the ice.

   B. Strong winds pushed them.

   C. All of the above.

OF QUARTZ I DO!

Find an antonym for each word in the text.

5. huge _____   rough _____

Measure the distance each rock traveled. Write the lengths.

(Scale: 1 cm is 10 m)

1. _____

_____ m

2. _____

_____ m

3. _____

_____ m

4. _____

_____ m

5. _____

_____ m

6. _____

_____ m

Follow the directions.

Read the clues and use the chart to figure out the weight of each rock.

- Karen is not the heaviest rock.

- Hortense's weight is a prime number.

- Layla's weight is more than Goldy's weight.

- Goldy's weight is a multiple of 10.

	164 lb.	250 lb.	457 lb.	318 lb.
KAREN				
HORTENSE				
LAYLA				
GOLDY				

Answer Key

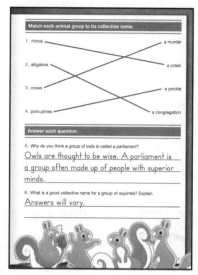

Page 5

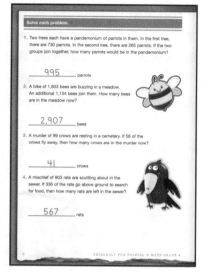

Page 6

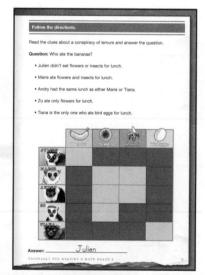

Page 7

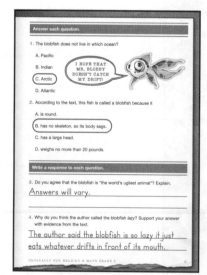

Page 9

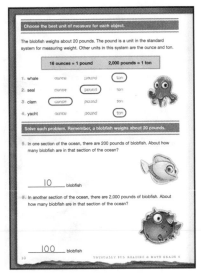

Page 10

Page 11

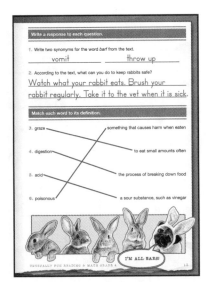

Page 13

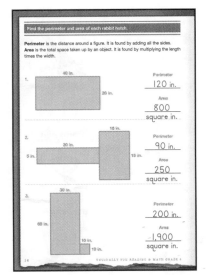

Page 14

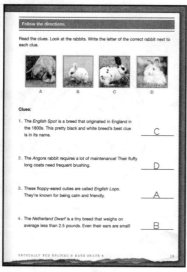

Page 15

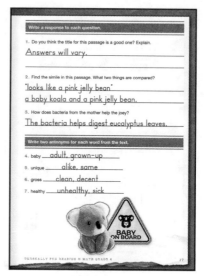

Page 17

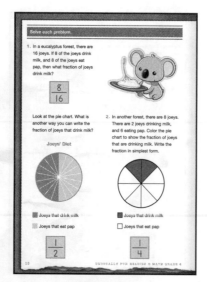

Page 18

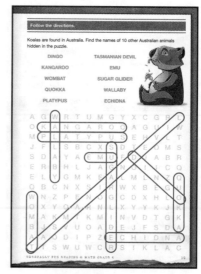

Page 19

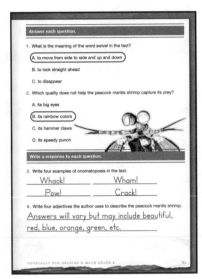

Page 21

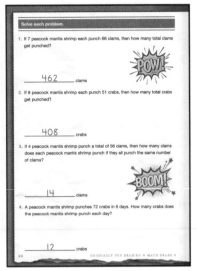

Page 22

Page 23

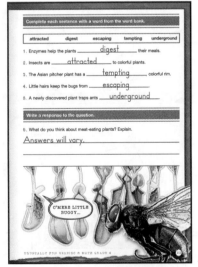

Page 25

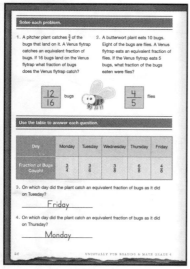

Page 26

Page 27

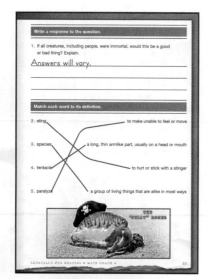

Page 29

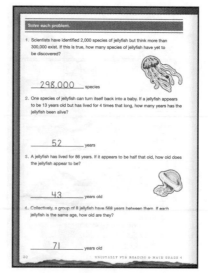

Page 30

Page 31

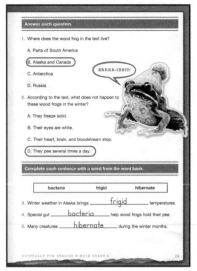

Page 33

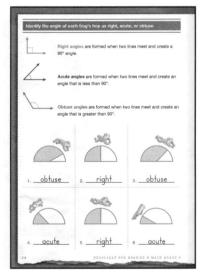

Page 34

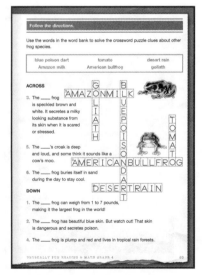

Page 35

Answer Key

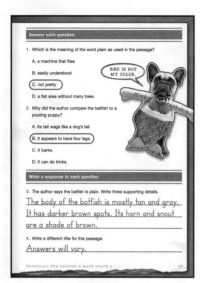

Page 37

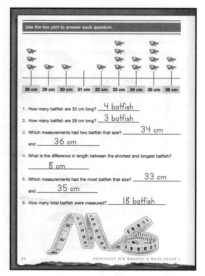

Page 38

Page 39

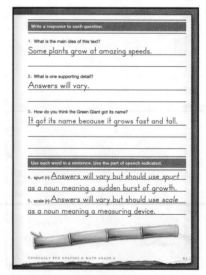

Page 41

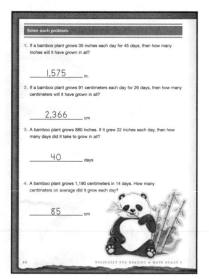

Page 42

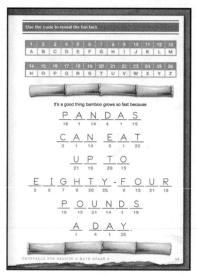

Page 43

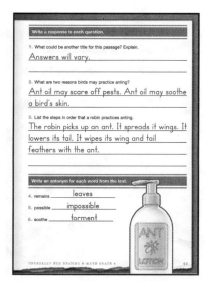

Page 45

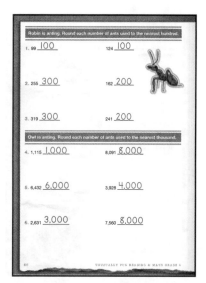

Page 46

Page 47

Follow the directions.

Help the ants find the bird! Write the letters the ants pass in order on the lines below to finish the fun fact.

Relative to their size, ants are one of the

S T R O N G E S T

creatures in the world. They can carry F I F T Y

times their body weight!

Page 49

Write a response to each question.

1. What two things does Yang want you to know about training goldfish?

First, let the goldfish get to know you. Second, reward them with food.

2. What are three soccer skills Yang trained his goldfish to do?

dribble   pass   score

Write two meanings for each word from the passage.

3. train

a connected line of railroad cars

to teach something

4. score

number of points each side has in a game

to make a basket, goal, or run in a sport

Page 50

Solve each problem.

(Hint: To find an average, add the quantities and then divide the sum by the number of quantities.)

1. On Monday, a goldfish touches the soccer ball 10 times. On Tuesday, the goldfish touches the ball 14 times. On Wednesday, the goldfish touches the ball 12 times. Find the average number of times the goldfish touches the ball.

12 times

2. A goldfish scores 2 goals on Saturday. On Sunday, the goldfish scores 5 goals. On Monday, the goldfish scores 3 goals. On Tuesday the goldfish scores 6 goals. Find the average number of goals the goldfish scores.

4 goals

3. A team of goldfish work on touching the ball. The team touches the ball 22 times in round one, 36 times in round two, 29 times in round three, 31 times in round four, and 32 times in round 5. What was the average number of times the team touched the ball?

30 times

GOAL!

Page 51

Use the code to reveal the fun fact.

1	2	3	4	5	6	7	8	9	10	11	12	13
A	B	C	D	E	F	G	H	I	J	K	L	M

14	15	16	17	18	19	20	21	22	23	24	25	26
N	O	P	Q	R	S	T	U	V	W	X	Y	Z

Goldfish C A N ' T
3 1 14 20

S H U T T H E I R
19 8 21 20 20 8 5 9 18

E Y E S .
5 25 5 19

T H E Y D O N ' T
20 8 5 25 4 15 14 20

H A V E
8 1 22 5

E Y E L I D S !
5 25 5 12 9 4 19

Page 53

Write a response to each question.

1. What does the author say might be a reason the secretary bird got its name? Support your answer with evidence from the text.

<u>Answers will vary.</u>

2. Connect what you read about the secretary bird to another bird or animal you have read about. Explain.

<u>Answers will vary.</u>

Answer the question.

3. Which of these statements tells the main idea of the third paragraph?

A. The secretary bird has large feet and sharp claws.

B. The secretary bird is quite vicious to its prey.

C. The secretary bird lives in Africa.

D. The secretary bird nests in a tree.

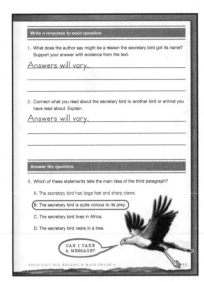

CAN I TAKE A MESSAGE?

Page 54

Complete the graph and answer each question.

A secretary bird had a week filled with snake hunting. The number of snakes the bird caught each day is listed below.

Sunday: 0 snakes
Monday: 1 snake
Tuesday: 3 snakes
Wednesday: 1 snake
Thursday: 2 snakes
Friday: 4 snakes
Saturday: 5 snakes

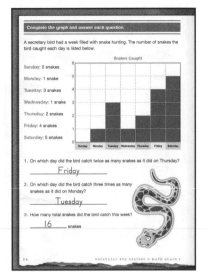

Snakes Caught

1. On which day did the bird catch twice as many snakes as it did on Thursday?

<u>Friday</u>

2. On which day did the bird catch three times as many snakes as it did on Monday?

<u>Tuesday</u>

3. How many total snakes did the bird catch this week?

<u>16</u> snakes

Page 55

Follow the directions.

Read each clue. Cross out the letters from the words *BIRDS OF PREY*. Write the remaining letters on the lines to reveal a bird of prey.

1. Tufts of feathers called *plumicorns* sit on this bird's head and are how it got its name.

GREAT HORNED OWL

2. This rare bird has a harsh habitat. It lives along the cold rocky coasts of eastern Russia.

STELLAR'S SEA-EAGLE

3. This bird lives in the Andes Mountain range and has the largest wingspan of any raptor.

ANDEAN CONDOR

4. These falcons are the fastest ever recorded animal, with a diving speed reaching 242 miles per hour.

PEREGRINE FALCON

5. If you've ever heard the caw of an eagle in a movie, odds are it is the actual scream of this colorful-tailed bird.

RED-TAILED HAWK

Page 57

Answer each question.

1. Ice-cream cone worms live

A. under rocks.

B. in cone-shaped tubes.

C. in seashells.

2. These worms can be found in

A. Central and South America.

B. North America.

C. Australia.

D. Iceland.

Write a response to each question.

3. The author said the worms "spend most of their lives facedown!" What did the author mean?

<u>These worms burrow headfirst into layers of</u> <u>sand and mud to find food.</u>

4. Draw an ice-cream cone worm in the box. Label it with adjectives from the text.

Drawings will vary and should be labeled with adjectives from the text.

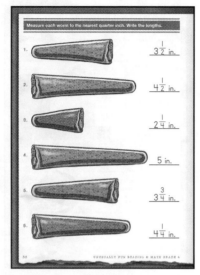

Page 58

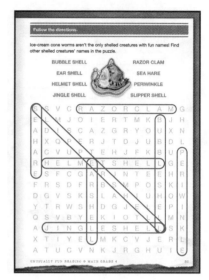

Page 59

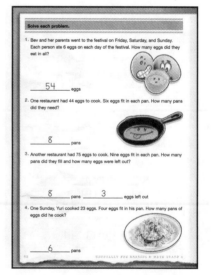

Page 61

Page 62

Page 63

Follow the directions.

George, Gina, and Gabby attended the festival. The restaurant mixed up their orders. Which order belongs to each person? Use the chart and the clues to find out!

- Gina ordered a number of eggs that is a factor of 14.
- Gabby ordered a number of eggs that is divisible by two.
- George ordered a number of eggs that is a square number.

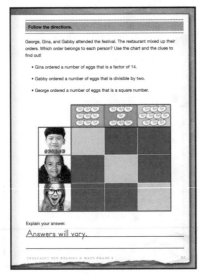

Explain your answer.

Answers will vary.

Page 65

Write a response to each question.

1. Why did the author title this passage "Joe's Green Thumb"? Is Joe's thumb actually green?

No, Joe's thumb is not green. "Green thumb" is a figure of speech meaning "good at gardening."

2. Why did the author say one plant's vine snaked around the shower?

The vine curved around the shower like a snake.

Match each word to its definition.

3. jungle — a place covered with trees, plants, and bushes

4. collection — green plants

5. greenery — to take in or out, secretly

6. smuggle — a group of gathered things that are alike

Page 66

Solve each problem.

1. If Joe spent $4,200 for all of his 1,400 plants, how much did each plant cost if he spent the same amount on each?

$ **3**

2. If Joe buys more plants and now has a total of 1,628 plants, how many did he buy (and sneak by his grandmother)?

228 plants

3. Joe waters each of his 1,400 plants once a week. How many plants get watered each day?

200 plants

Complete the table. Answer the question.

4. Joe buys the same number of plants each year.

Year 1	250 plants
Year 2	500 plants
Year 3	750 plants
Year 4	1,000 plants
Year 5	1,250 plants

5. If Joe continued to buy plants in this pattern, during which year would he reach his current total of 1,400 plants?

Year **6**

Page 67

Follow the directions.

Help Joe find his dog! Follow the path of problems whose answers are odd.

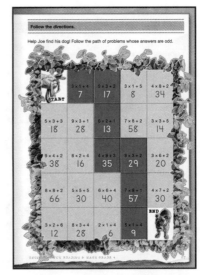

Answer Key

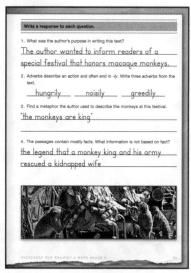

Page 69

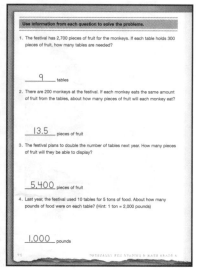

Page 70

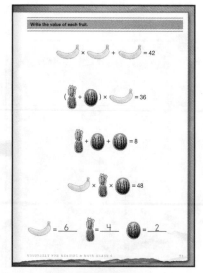

Page 71

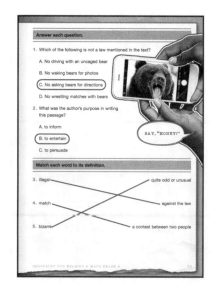

Page 73

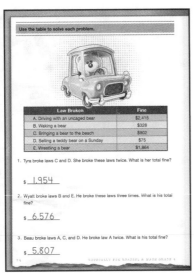

Page 74

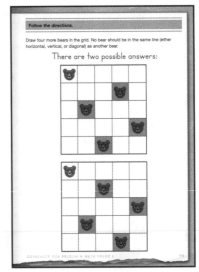

Page 75

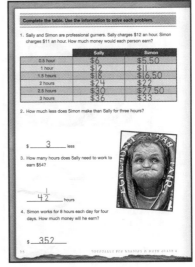

Page 77

Page 78

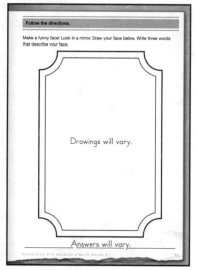

Page 79

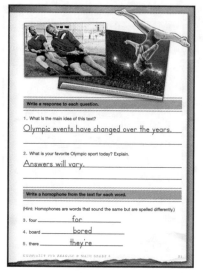

Page 81

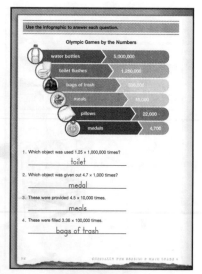

Page 82

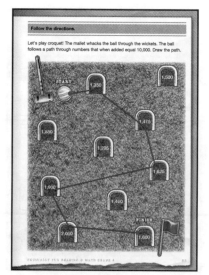

Page 83

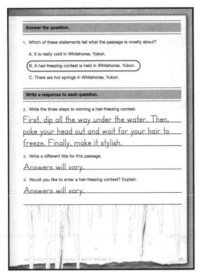

Page 85

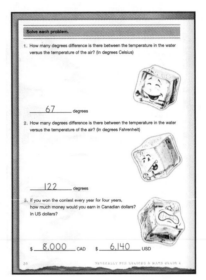

Page 86

Page 87

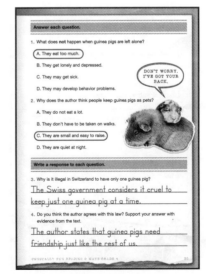

Page 89

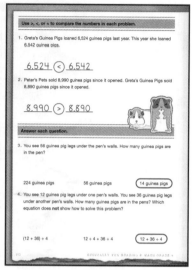

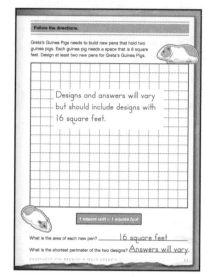

Page 90

Page 91

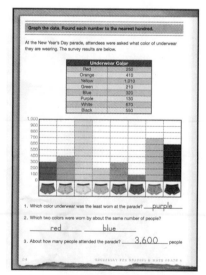

Page 93

Page 94

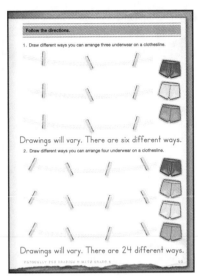

Page 95

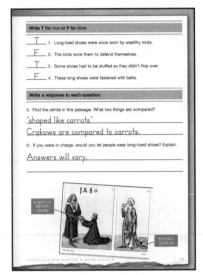

Page 97

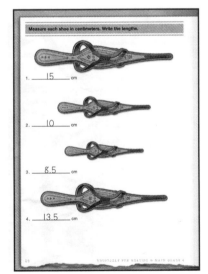

Page 98

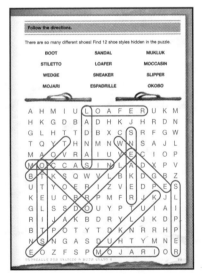

Page 99

Page 101

Answer each question.

1. What was the author's purpose in writing this passage?

   (A.) to inform

   B. to entertain

   C. to persuade

2. Which statement is **not** true about the house kits?

   A. The kits contained everything needed to build a house.

   B. Family, friends, and neighbors helped put the house together.

   (C.) The houses were delivered on big trucks.

   D. The kits were shipped by railroad.

Write a response to the question.

3. If you could buy a house kit today, what features would you want? Write 3–5 sentences describing the kit.

   Answers will vary.

Page 102

Solve each problem.

1. The Mabe family wants to buy a house kit for $1,320. If the family saves $40 a month, how many months will they need to save to buy the kit?

   __33__ months

2. The Smith family wants to buy a house kit for $624. If the family saves $12 a week, how many weeks will they need to save to buy the kit? About how many months is that?

   __52__ weeks __12__ months

3. New Town wants to purchase a school kit for $10,800. Last year the town raised $4,930. How much more do they need to raise to buy the school kit?

   $ __5,870__

4. Acme Builders wants to buy 12 house kits for their housing development. If each kit costs $410, how much will they spend on kits?

   $ __4,920__

5. The Johnson family saved some money to buy a kit. They need to save $128 more to buy the $1,150 kit. How much have they saved so far?

   $ __1,022__

Page 103

Follow the directions.

Draw the missing houses so that each color of house appears only once in each row, column, or square.

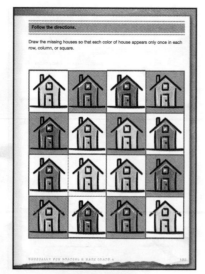

Page 105

Write a response to each question.

1. What is the main idea of the passage?

   Ancient Egyptians cared a lot about how they looked.

2. Identify two key details that support the main idea.

   Accept any two: Both men and women wore makeup. They used almond oil to condition their hair. They scrubbed themselves with sea salt. They plucked out body hair with tweezers.

Match each word to its definition.

3. malachite — a bright green stone

4. kohl — black eyeliner

5. galena — a dark gray mineral

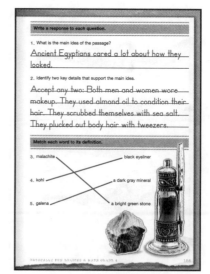

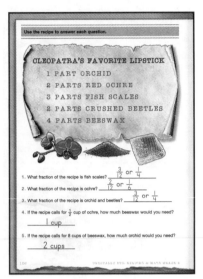

Page 106

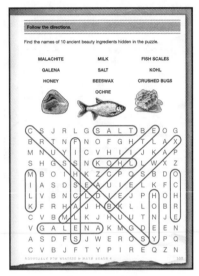

Page 107

Page 109

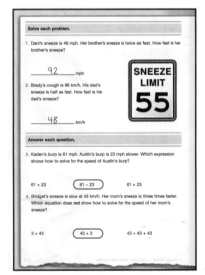

Page 110

Answer Key

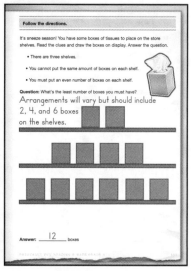

Follow the directions.

It's sneeze season! You have some boxes of tissues to place on the store shelves. Read the clues and draw the boxes on display. Answer the question.

- There are three shelves.
- You cannot put the same amount of boxes on each shelf.
- You must put an even number of boxes on each shelf.

Question: What's the least number of boxes you must have?

Arrangements will vary but should include 2, 4, and 6 boxes on the shelves.

Answer: __12__ boxes

Page 111

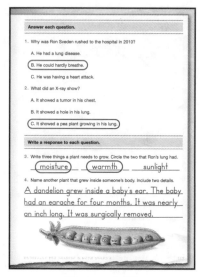

Answer each question.

1. Why was Ron Sveden rushed to the hospital in 2010?

   A. He had a lung disease.

   B. He could hardly breathe. ⟵ circled

   C. He was having a heart attack.

2. What did an X-ray show?

   A. It showed a tumor in his chest.

   B. It showed a hole in his lung.

   C. It showed a pea plant growing in his lung. ⟵ circled

Write a response to each question.

3. Write three things a plant needs to grow. Circle the two that Ron's lung had.

   (moisture)   (warmth)   sunlight

4. Name another plant that grew inside someone's body. Include two details.

   A dandelion grew inside a baby's ear. The baby had an earache for four months. It was nearly an inch long. It was surgically removed.

Page 113

Use the table to answer each question.

Plant Growth

Day	Height in Inches
1	0.25
2	0.50
3	1
4	2

1. If a pea plant continues to grow in the same pattern, about how many inches tall will it be on day 6?

   __8__ in.

2. If a pea plant continues to grow in the same pattern, on what day would it reach 16 inches?

   Day __7__

3. If a pea plant continues to grow in the same pattern, about how many inches tall will it be on day 9?

   __64__ in.

4. If a pea plant continues to grow in the same pattern, on what day would it reach 128 inches?

   Day __10__

Page 114

Use the code to reveal the fun fact.

1	2	3	4	5	6	7	8	9	10	11	12	13
A	B	C	D	E	F	G	H	I	J	K	L	M

14	15	16	17	18	19	20	21	22	23	24	25	26
N	O	P	Q	R	S	T	U	V	W	X	Y	Z

A similar case as Ron's occurred in 2009. A Russian man had this type of plant growing inside his lung. He also made a full recovery.

A
1

F I R
6 9 18

T R E E
20 18 5 5

Page 115

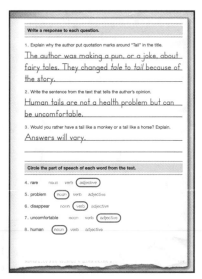

Page 117

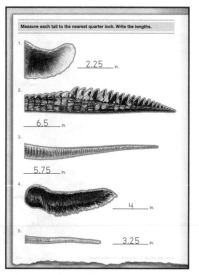

Page 118

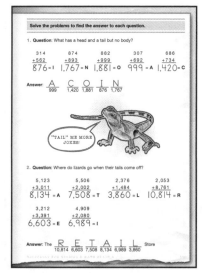

Page 119

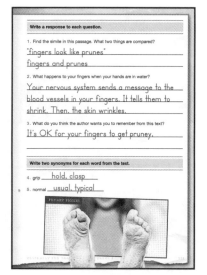

Page 121

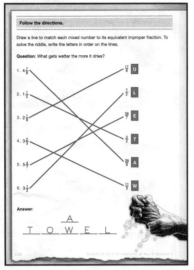

Page 122

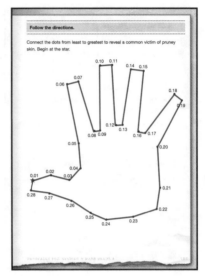

Page 123

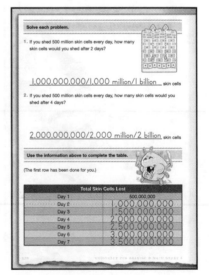

Page 125

Page 126

Answer Key

Page 127

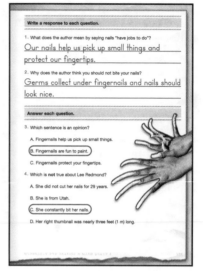

Page 129

Page 130

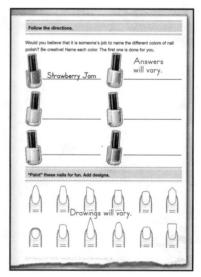

Page 131

Page 133

Write a response to each question.

1. Name two things on display at a Virginia museum.
a ham that is 120 years old
a peanut found in 1890

2. Would you eat a chunk of this old ham? Explain.
Answers will vary.

Write two different meanings for each word from the passage.

3. safe
free from harm
strong metal box to keep valuables in

4. sports
athletic games
displays or shows off

5. cured
to make healthy
to preserve with salt or smoke

Page 134

Solve each problem.

1. Rover's favorite Saturday activity is watching the HAM CAM. He started watching it at 2:30 p.m. If he watched it for 1 hour 35 minutes, what time did he stop?

4:05 p.m.

2. Lady watched the HAM CAM from 11:15 a.m. to 12:45 p.m. How long did Lady watch the HAM CAM?

$1\frac{1}{2}$ hours or 1 hour, 30 minutes

3. Binky and Dinky stopped watching the Ham Cam at 6:05 p.m. They watched for a total of 2 hours and 10 minutes. What time did Binky and Dinky start watching the HAM CAM?

3:55 p.m.

4. Fluff and Nutter both watched the same amount of HAM CAM yesterday. Fluff started at 10:30 a.m. and stopped at 2:55 p.m. Nutter started at 9:20 a.m. What time did he stop watching the HAM CAM?

1:45 p.m.

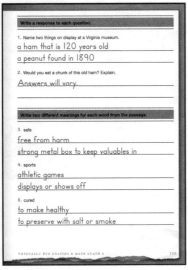

Page 135

Follow the directions.

The year that each food item was purchased is on each label. Write how old each food item is based on the current year.

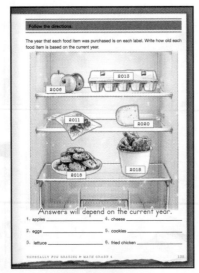

Answers will depend on the current year.

1. apples _____   4. cheese _____

2. eggs _____   5. cookies _____

3. lettuce _____   6. fried chicken _____

Page 137

Complete each sentence with a word from the word bank.

dashed	highways	lanes	solid

1. Most __highways__ have lines dividing them into two or more __lanes__

2. Some of the lines are __solid__, meaning you can't pass.

3. Other lines are __dashed__, meaning you can pass if it's safe.

Write a response to each question.

4. What was Edward Hines's big idea and what was the result?
Edward Hines saw a milk wagon leaking milk on the road. It led him to think about using white lines for traffic safety. Soon, there were lines on many highways.

5. Most roads have white lines along each side. What do you think they are for?
Answers may vary but should in some way say that they are there to show drivers where the road surface ends.

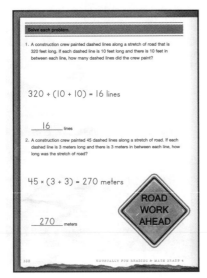

Page 138

Solve each problem.

1. A construction crew painted dashed lines along a stretch of road that is 320 feet long. If each dashed line is 10 feet long and there is 10 feet in between each line, how many dashed lines did the crew paint?

320 ÷ (10 + 10) = 16 lines

___16___ lines

2. A construction crew painted 45 dashed lines along a stretch of road. If each dashed line is 3 meters long and there is 3 meters in between each line, how long was the stretch of road?

45 × (3 + 3) = 270 meters

___270___ meters

ROAD WORK AHEAD

Page 139

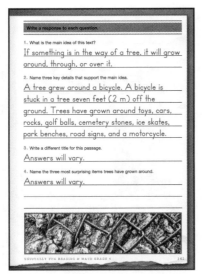

Page 141

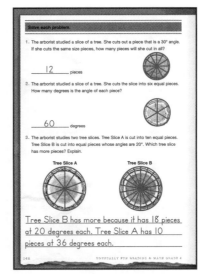

Page 142

Page 143

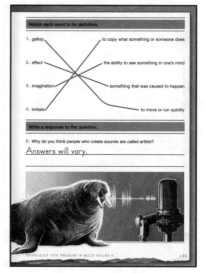

Page 145

Page 146

Page 147

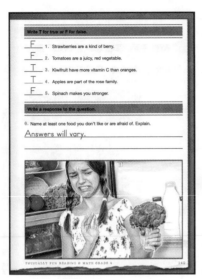

Page 149

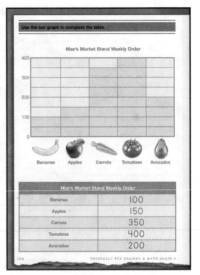

Page 150

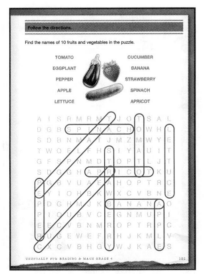

Page 151

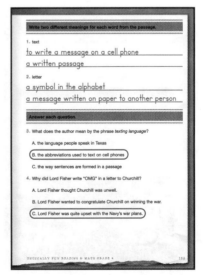

Page 153

Answer Key

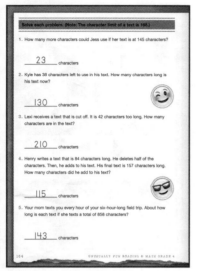

Page 154

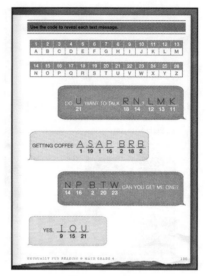

Page 155

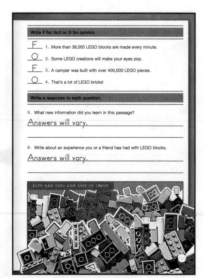

Page 157

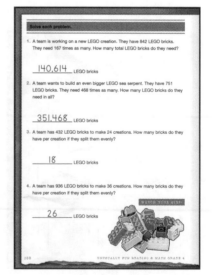

Page 158

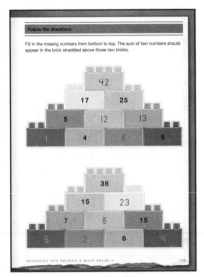

Page 159

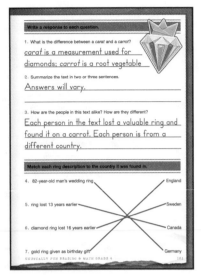

Page 161

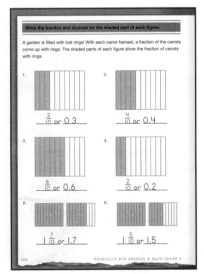

Page 162

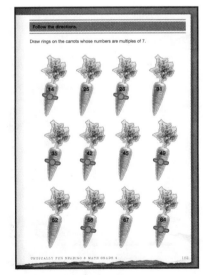

Page 163

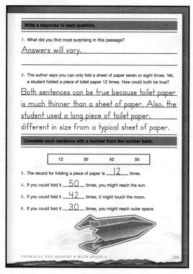

Page 165

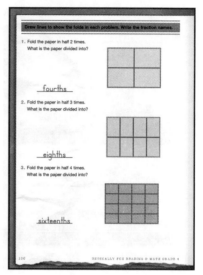

Page 166

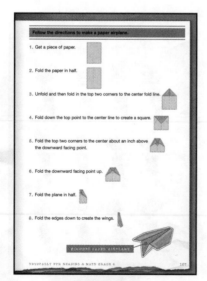

Page 167

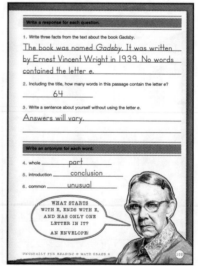

Page 169

Answer Key

Page 170

Page 171

Page 173

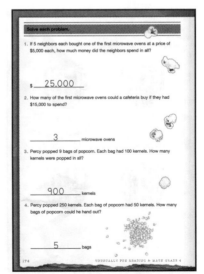

Page 174

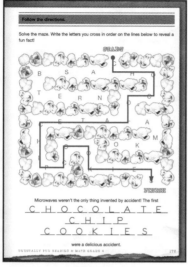

Page 175

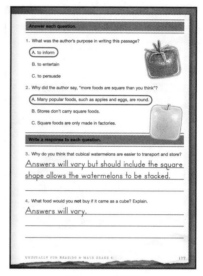

Page 177

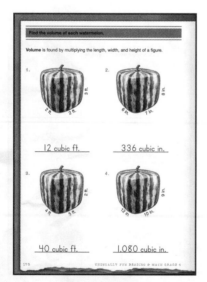

Page 178

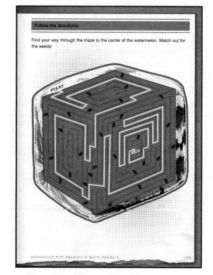

Page 179

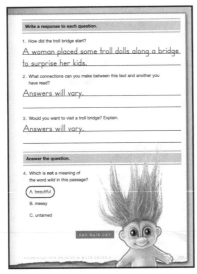

Page 181

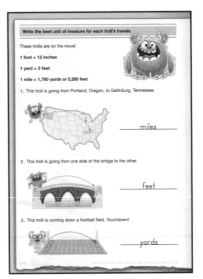

Page 182

Use the code to reveal the fun fact.

Take a hike in Breckenridge, Colorado, if you'd like to come face-to-face with a

15-foot-tall W O O D E N   T R O L L !

The hiking trail is called the

T R O L L S T I G E N

T R A I L and the T R O L L ' S

N A M E   I S

I S A K

H E A R T S T O N E

Page 183

Page 185

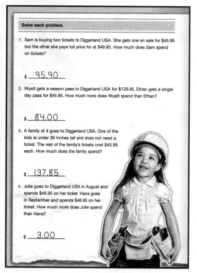

Page 186

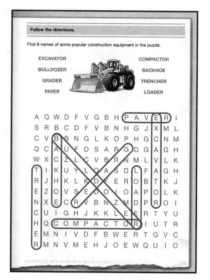

Page 187

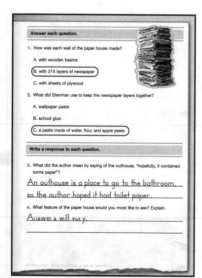

Page 189

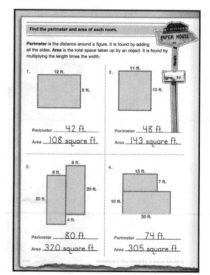

Page 190

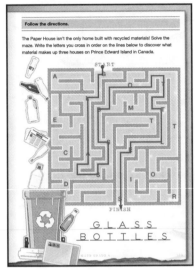

Page 191

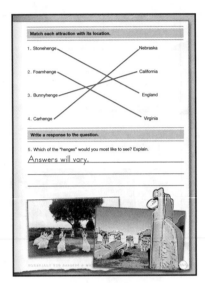

Page 193

Page 194

Page 195

Answer Key

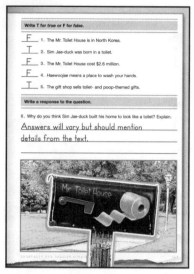

Page 198

Answer each question.

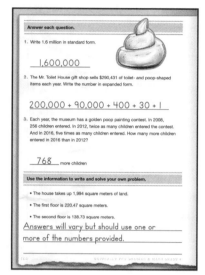

1. Write 1.6 million in standard form.

1,600,000

2. The Mr. Toilet House gift shop sells $290,431 of toilet- and poop-shaped items each year. Write the number in expanded form.

200,000 + 90,000 + 400 + 30 + 1

3. Each year, the museum has a golden poop painting contest. In 2008, 256 children entered. In 2012, twice as many children entered the contest. And in 2016, five times as many children entered. How many more children entered in 2016 than in 2012?

768 more children

Use the information to write and solve your own problem.

- The house takes up 1,994 square meters of land.
- The first floor is 220.47 square meters.
- The second floor is 138.73 square meters.

Answers will vary but should use one or more of the numbers provided.

Page 199

Follow the directions.

Cross out every other letter in each toilet name. Write the remaining letters on the lines. Then, write the circled letters in order to answer the question. The first one has been done for you.

1. P~A~R~O~I~O~V~E~Y   P R I V Y

2. J~H~O~O~I~H~N   J O H N

3. L~O~A~N~T~R~A~I~N~E   L A T R I N E

4. L~E~O~O~V~O~Y   L O O

5. C~T~O~M~M~M~O~D~F~E~L   C O M M O D E

6. P~R~O~L~T~E~T~Y~V   P O T T Y

Question: What did one toilet say to the other?

Answer: Y O u   L O O k

A LI T T LE FLUSHED!

Page 201

Write a response to each question.

1. Describe The Gum Wall in Seattle, Washington.

The Gum Wall is a 50-foot wall of a theater building where thousands of people have stuck their chewing gum.

2. Write two reasons why gum is against the law in Singapore.

Gum is litter. Birds can die from eating it. People get shoes stuck in it. Gum lasts forever.

3. Do you think The Gum Wall is fun or gross? Explain.

Answers will vary.

Use each word in a sentence. Use the part of speech indicated.

4. wad (n) Answers will vary but must include the correct use of the noun "wad."

5. attraction (n) Answers will vary but must include the correct use of the noun "attraction."

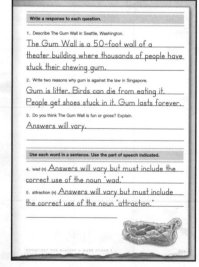

Page 202

Solve each problem.

1. It took workers 130 hours to remove 2,350 pounds of gum. About how many pounds of gum were removed each hour?

18 pounds

2. If 5,000 new wads of gum are added to the wall each year from 1990 to the current year, how many wads of gum are there now?

Answers will vary.

_____ wads

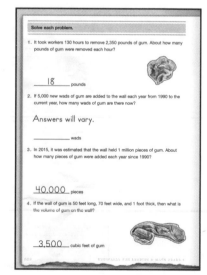

3. In 2015, it was estimated that the wall held 1 million pieces of gum. About how many pieces of gum were added each year since 1990?

40,000 pieces

4. If the wall of gum is 50 feet long, 70 feet wide, and 1 foot thick, then what is the volume of gum on the wall?

3,500 cubic feet of gum

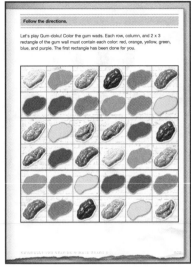

Page 203

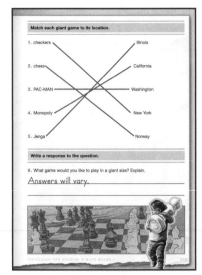

Page 205

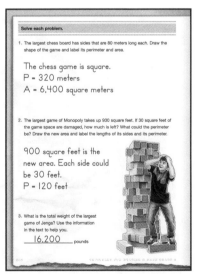

Page 206

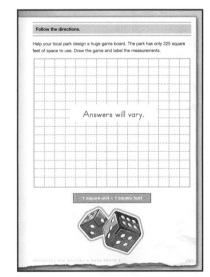

Page 207

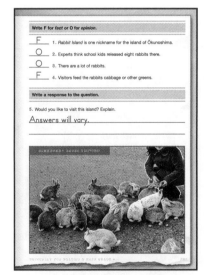

Page 209

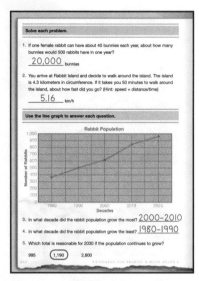

Page 210

Page 211

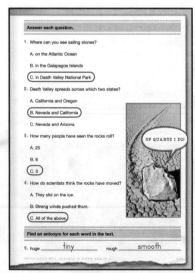

Page 213

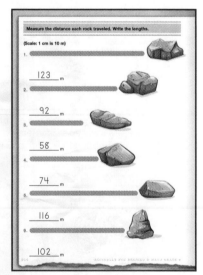

Page 214

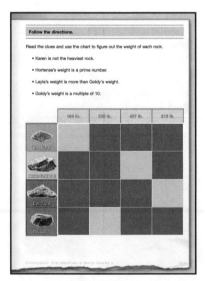

Page 215